The Norfolk Bedside Book

The Norfolk Bedside Book

chosen and edited by

Keith Skipper

The Norfolk Bedside Book

Introduction and selection © Keith Skipper 2002

First published in 2002 by
Mousehold Press
Victoria Cottage
Constitution Opening
Norwich, NR3 4BD

Cover photograph: Sue Mullard

Illustrations: Sam Robbins

ISBN 1 874739 21 8

Printed by Watkiss Studios Ltd., Biggleswade

OTHER BOOKS BY KEITH SKIPPER

Keith Skipper's many books about Norfolk include the following:

Dew Yew Keep a'Troshin'!,1984,
Down at The Datty Duck, 1985
Dunt Fergit Ter Hevver Larf, 1986
(Old Barney's broadcasts on BBC Radio Norfolk, all published by Jim Baldwin, Fakenham.)
A Load of Old Squit, Jim Baldwin, 1985
A Norfolk Logbook, Jim Baldwin, 1986
Naturally Norfolk (with artist Ken Walton), Jim Baldwin, 1988
The Norfolk Connection, Poppyland Publishing, 1992
More Norfolk Connections, Poppyland Publishing, 1992
The Norfolk Companion, Jim Baldwin, 1994
Squit, Wit and...Shifty Tales!, Nostalgia Publications, 1995
Larn Yarself Norfolk, Nostalgia Publications, 1996
Village Post, Nostalgia Publications, 1996
Rustic Revels (with cartoonist Tony Hall), Nostalgia Publications, 1997
Skipper's Byways, Eastern Daily Press, 1998
Hidden Norfolk, Countryside Books, 1998
Farewell My Bewty (with photographer Sam Robbins), Mousehold Press, 1999
Broad Smiles, Lathams, Potter Heigham, 2000
Hev Yew Gotta Loight, Boy?, Countryside Books, 2001

To all who have pushed a pen
to serve the Norfolk cause.

CONTENTS

The leaves of the elms are coming down in showers, lawns and flower-beds are littered, and the marks of the threshing machines are pressed in the new mud of the lane. It is comforting to sit by a fire that roars with the passing of the wind over the chimney, but how quickly has the year fled away.

Lilias Rider Haggard, *Norfolk Life*, 1943

INTRODUCTION

It's a bit like being asked to choose your own team for an important confrontation in a packed school playground. Pleasure at landing the role of chief selector has to be tempered by immediate acceptance that several worthy candidates are bound to be overlooked.

I have tried to be fair, to assemble a balanced line-up to do justice to Norfolk's outstanding reputation for inspiring good writing and to my long-standing passion for applauding it. But, of course, I am as susceptible as the next playground picker to the coy wink, knowing smile, timely nudge, and friendly wave .....

Still, if such attention-seeking ploys simply serve to pin-point obvious talents, my selection qualities surely ought to be allowed a reasonable run. There's nothing wrong in showing favouritism if subsequent results are favourable. I think this collection will fully vindicate me.

Several automatic choices started asking to be noticed well over 40 years ago when I first discovered the qualities of home-spun authors like Jonathan Mardle (splendid pseudonym of *Eastern Daily Press* essayist and leader writer Eric Fowler), Sidney Grapes, creator of the evergreen Boy John dialect letters, and Ted Ellis, the people's naturalist whose enthusiasm and expertise shone through every paragraph.

They whetted my appetite to seek out painters with words from an earlier Norfolk canvas – rural realism novelists Mary Mann and James Blyth, scholarly parson Augustus Jessopp and Henry Rider Haggard, the romancer of King Solomon's Mines who became a gentleman farmer on the Norfolk–Suffolk border. His youngest daughter, Lilias, inherited that marvellous gift for wielding a potent pen, and she has emerged as one of my favourite contributors to a rich tapestry of local literature.

My seventeen years as a full-time journalist on our local newspapers, and fifteen years as a regular broadcaster on BBC

Radio Norfolk brought constant opportunities to meet writers great and small, many of them with deep roots in this corner of the world.

From Booker Prize contenders to village history compilers, they all revelled in that exciting tingle of creation which accompanies something new in print. Shelves packed with signed copies of books about the county bear testimony as to how an interest burgeoned into a compulsion. Happily, many writers still send me copies of their latest works.

Playwright Arnold Wesker, who put Norfolk on an international stage with *Roots*, allowed me to add my own parochial touches to a dialogue between two farmworkers putting their backs into it, up and down the sugar beet rows. Wesker wrote it in 1953 when knockin' and toppin' were still in fashion. It had to wait until 1984 for a world premiere on Radio Norfolk and a place for posterity in my volume, *Skipper's Logbook*.

Malcolm Bradbury, driving spirit behind the world-famous creative writing course at the University of East Anglia, was the most accessible of academics. I interviewed him many times on all kinds of literary topics, and he was impressed by the quantity and quality of work inspired by Norfolk –

> ...a place of relative peace and a sense of being almost at the edge of things. It affords me a distance on the literary and media world and its smart and international values, a kind of common sense.

The amiable professor freely admitted he knew little of neglected Norfolk writers like Mary Mann and James Blyth. 'We leave them to people like you,' he smiled. I took that as a supreme compliment as well as a cue to continue campaigning to bring them to the fore.

I have been happy to renew countless other friendships in the pages of this miscellany, not least with prolific poets Edward Storey and John Kett. Both proved outstandingly generous in their support – Edward from a comparatively new base: the Fenland champion moved from his spiritual flatlands to the foot of ancient hills in North Wales. 'I am a born-again poet, gaining much more by seeing the Fens from a distance, both in time and space,' he said, on sending me a copy of his *New and Selected Poems*. Several are included in this volume as he continues to 'sing my song in a strange land.'

To all others gathered here whom I have met, in person or merely in print, sincere thanks for splendid company over the years. Special nods of gratitude towards Sam Robbins, for telling illustrations at the head of each section; to publisher, Adrian Bell for cheery encouragement over all hurdles; and to my wife Diane for yet another stirring stint at the word processor while I hid behind thousands of pages.

As the winds of change continue to rail against our Norfolk windows, this collection must provide end-of-day reassurance to native and newcomer alike. We can still be rich while keeping our distance.

Keith Skipper
Cromer, 2002

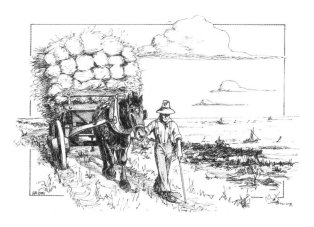

WORKING LAND AND SEA

It is often claimed Norfolk people have one foot on the land and the other in the sea. Certainly, there's still mutual respect among those who earn livings along the furrow or over the foam, even though numbers are dwindling dramatically in both cases.

This selection, inevitably, carries the air of an elegy for worlds of work either gone or fast disappearing. The march of mechanisation spells a different kind of horsepower across agri-business acres, while the continuing decline of our fishing industry asks serious questions of EEC policies as they affect a county all but surrounded by water.

Remember, it's all too easy to be nostalgic about a past you didn't have to live through. I have chosen carefully to avoid sentimental pitfalls, although the old camaraderie and pride in making much of little are evident.

Henry Williamson at Stiffkey and A Norfolk Woman (Lucilla Reeve) on the Battle Area in Breckland strive to keep the farming flag unfurled in wartime. Scottish fishergirls show how amazingly nimble fingers can sort out Silver Darlings. International playwright Arnold Wesker, with far less dexterity, makes a drama out of knockin' and toppin' sugar beet. Not much romance to spare there!

Part of Old England

As I came down from Fox Covert, my bare arms red with barley-beard scratches, I saw the family sitting down to tea on the triangle of grass before the big barn.

When I came here first, the grass everywhere was foul with thistles, nettles, burdocks, and other weeds. Bit by bit the weeds have been removed, and in their place the wild-white clover is beginning to spread itself. The grassy triangle before the barn was now almost free of weed, and pleasant to sit upon.

Around the plot of grass lay the new roads, gleaming chalky-yellow in the sun. Near by was the chalk quarry, shaded by tall trees. I had worked hard in the harvest field, and could observe with the eyes of a clear conscience, the jackdaws flying to their nests in the quarry, and in the holes and ledges behind the festoons of ivy and other hanging plants. But soon I found myself thinking, not in terms of wild-bird nesting, but of the best way to bring down about a thousand tons of that chalk, to spread it over the arable and the grass, to sweeten the soil, counter any acid which crippled the growth of such plants as clover and sugar-beet.

A large cup of tea was a welcome sight. I lay at ease beside the children, and began to munch a piece of cake. It was a plum cake, made of brown wholemeal flour ground in one of the last windmills of East Anglia – which meant one of the last in England: for what the rest of England had abandoned, East Anglia, and particularly Norfolk, was still using. I had liked Norfolk because it was part of Old England. Thus the four fat pink pigs, snouting in the clover a few feet away from our little family party, had been part of Old England, until, after much argument, they had been given freedom to roam wheresoever they wished.

*　　*　　*　　*　　*

It was pleasant to see the children in the harvest field. They led the horses to the stack, and frolicked around us during lunch and tea. We worked twelve hours during the fine weather.

Anxiously we watched dark thunder clouds moving around us, now over the sea, now over the distant horizon. But we were lucky: no tempest fell upon us. Some farms a few miles away lost much of their corn, beaten down by terrific hail-storms, which killed half-grown lambs, shattered plants of sugar-beet and mangold, and stripped hundreds of acres of standing barley.

Henry Williamson, *The Story of a Norfolk Farm*, 1941

Silver Darlings

My first visit to the Court of King Herring had been arranged by my parents as part of a scheme to widen my knowledge in preparation for my forthcoming scholarship exam. Far from being a mere educational chore, however, it proved such a fascination that I returned on every possible occasion. Now, looking back on those halcyon days, it is difficult to recall which aspect of the industry made the greatest impact on my young mind. I had, of course, seen a lot of the fishermen of Cromer and Sheringham, but the hurly-burly of the Yarmouth quay-side was like a different world.

Few who have ever seen the steady line of drifters putting to sea will readily forget the way in which each in succession would rise to meet the swell at the harbour bar. Then, after a hard night seeking out the Silver Darlings, they would return, heavily laden, in a mad dash to unload as quickly as possible in the hope of gaining the highest prices. It was what followed next, however, which aroused in me the greatest feeling of excitement. Cran after cran was lifted from the hold and dropped on the quay, the auctioneer's bell would ring, and both fish and men seemed to be everywhere whilst, up above, seagulls wheeled and screeched in the hope of a succulent meal. It was all conducted in accordance with a long-established routine but, to the uninitiated, it seemed sheer bedlam.

A short distance away, standing at a row of huge shallow troughs, the Fisher Girls went to work on that part of the catch which was destined for export. With their fingers separately bandaged for protection and wearing large black oilskin aprons, they split and gutted the herring and then, without even looking round, flung each one backwards with unerring aim into the waiting barrels behind them. They worked at a tremendous pace, each woman being capable of gutting at least a thousand fish in an hour. One could only stand and marvel at the speed and skill of the operation and, as the troughs emptied, so the men poured in more basketsful in a seemingly never-ending supply.

Bob Bagshaw, *Norfolk Remembered*, 1989

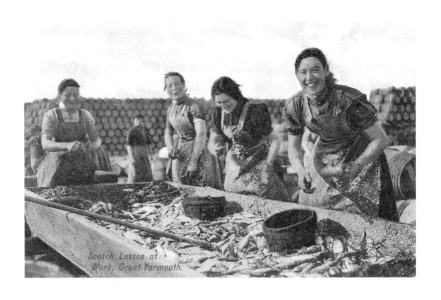

Scottish fishergirls gutting herring; Great Yarmouth

Survivor

Black on black,
the colour deepens beyond the day
to show another world held back
upon the furrowed page when earth
was wrinkled more by water than the plough,
where men expressed themselves in breath
heaved into air by limbs that knew
no other comfort than the sleep
which entered into them with night.

Today one man survives to show
how time has passed him by,
almost forgotten him within the light
that filters from a sky grown old
with watching. So burdened now with pain
he does not raise an eye
or lift his head from toil
to see what caused the shadow
darkening the soil.

Below the level of the dyke,
where water glistens closer to the sun
than his moist eye can reach,
he bends over the spade's clogged hilt,
his braces strained across his back
with all the tautness of a catapult.
But he's too solid and root-fixed
to know the joy of stone
shot briefly out of sight.

He is both past and present,
birth and death, the blood and spittle
of ten thousand years that raised
his place in history from beast -
to what? Should we regret
his breath has done no more
than leave an image on our winter sky
of what is certain for us all -
the shadow of a horseman passing by?

Edward Storey, 1995

Handsome Harry

Harry Gurnard, on the day on which Sally Smith hired Lifeboat House on behalf of Mrs. Dence, was probably the handsomest man within a five-mile radius of Holmhithe. He had gone to sea as a smack's boy as soon as ever the fatuous school regulations permitted, and although he missed that instinctive sense of weather and the whereabouts of fish which only comes to them who have learnt their craft from the age of seven or eight, he had the name of being a lucky man to have aboard a trawler. His atavism and his personal inclinations soon enabled him to forget whatever good or evil he may have learnt from the national schoolmasters, and at the age of twenty-five, when we first meet him, he could manage to sign his name, but any other literary effort 'made his hid ache.'

He had never travelled on a railway train in his life, and, save for his seafaring to north and west and south, he had never been ten miles away from his native village of Southam Score. But he was a man, one of the survivals of the time when all the fishermen along the coast of Daneshire, longshoremen and all, were men, before the horrible taint of the summer visitor had converted seamen and fishermen to cadging chairmen, or loafers on sixpenny sickers. Of his generation I have no hesitation in saying that he was, and is, the finest specimen of his race that I know – and that is high praise for a member of a race which includes probably the only, and certainly the most splendid, specimens of the old mixture of Danish or Scandinavian blood with the original blood of the Iceni of Daneshire. A magnificent, upstanding man of six feet one, his shoulders, beneath his jersey and oily overall, must have measured close on to fifty-five inches round his chest (for hot or cold the east-coast fishermen will wear five or six inches of clothing about him when he goes to sea). His strong, straight features suggested that, in addition to the blood already named, he may have had a strain of Norman descent in him; and his huge eyes, of deep sea-blue beneath a clear sky were fringed and emphasised by his dark brown hair, brows and lashes. He wore a moustache, but did not imitate his fathers in retaining the rim of bristly hair beneath his chin from ear to ear – that hirsute dewlap so dear to the old men of the coast. His mouth was full-lipped, and rather large than small, but his lips were kindly curved, and even when he was drunk he was never brutal. The boys who had sailed with him always spoke well of him, and loved him (as well as school had left it in them to love any man) with the honest, hearty love of comradeship. And the girls – well, naturally, whether they appreciated his good points to the full or no, they were all eager after him.

James Blyth, *A Longshore Lass*, 1910

Unlucky thirteenth

1941 was my last harvest, just as I felt it would be; and again on the thirteenth of June, a year after the 'Powers that Were' struck what then seemed a pretty bad blow, came news that made the other fade into insignificance. Eighteen thousand acres were wanted for army training and eight thousand of it was part of the estate I was managing. I was to lose not only my farm but my home cottage and the estate office at the duck farm as well. It was indeed a blow, for although I had lately wondered if they would take all land south of the Tottington-Stanford road, I'd never dreamed they would take the whole of Tottington village and parts of Thompson and Merton. Now I'd have nowhere to live and where could I go with my farming stock and two houses of furniture? Where was everyone to go? It was not the job of the army to re-house us – the Local Authorities had to do that, and with everywhere full of evacuees, it was going to be difficult.

One of the worst things about that first week was the rumour that it wasn't going to happen after all ... somebody had found the site wasn't suitable, we hadn't to move out. How I could have slain the people responsible for those lying tales; for every few hours one tenant or another would telephone or call to know from me, their agent, if it was true we hadn't to move? I am afraid, until some of them got the requisition notices, they did not believe it was true. Although secretly many preparations had been made, a lot of forms could not be dealt with until owners and tenants were told of the news. We were told on the thirteenth and requisition took place on the twentieth – seven days, and they actually thought we could all be moved in that time! Eventually we were given until the eighteenth of July; and I can only think of those five weeks as hell let loose.

In some ways we were in a worse plight than people who had lost their homes from enemy bombs; and we did not get the sympathy we would have had under those circumstances. We still had our goods and chattels, and homes were to be found for us – it said so in the papers! Then, too, we were to be generously compensated – they said so in the House of Commons! In fact, there were many who almost brutally told us we should make a fortune out of the move. If ever they have to go through anything of that kind, they will then realise how cruel and heartless such remarks were. As the Psalmist said, '… had it been an enemy who had done this thing…' we should have had a chance of defending our homes – we were pretty well organised as regards invasion, etc., and we'd have defended our land to the last ditch. Now we were just more evacuees needing shelter.

Lucilla Reeve, *Farming on a Battle Ground*, 1950

Resolute wives

The fishermen's wives had to be just as resolute and strong and hardworking. Alone they'd have the responsibility of the family. If their boat was late home there was no way of knowing why, only if another boat saw one in trouble would there be aid. The wives would clean mussels for baiting lines, gut herrings to be dried, bloatered or kippered. They'd have to souse jars and jars of herrings for their own consumption. There would be days or weeks on end without money coming in. They would have to have a stewpot on the fire with hot nourishing food for whenever the men got home. They'd have to have wet jerseys, slops, trousers and oilskins and boots drying and airing by their fires. After days of washing and drying wet seagoing clothes and countless sets of underwear and socks I look at the automatic machine and winder with awe. How in heaven's name did my predecessors manage? They would sit and knit stockings, mittens and ganseys in their spare time. Ah! those were the days! They'd hardly have time to spare to stand watching and worrying. I think over the years they'd have developed a telepathy and instinctively knew what was happening out of sight. I've experienced this myself. I expect most married couples sharing a good life together can develop such a rapport. In these days of radio and T.V., engines, winches, spindryers, and synthetics so much of the old knowledge goes, not needed any longer. A fisherman with the love of the sea in his veins is only truly happy when he's on it. If adverse conditions make it dangerous at times his adrenalin is high and this excitement is what its all about. It's a fever that's catching and I for one can instinctively know when I need to worry and when worry or fear is unwarranted.

Katherine Lee, *Crabs and Shannocks*, 1983

Cottage farmers

Roughly speaking, the ex-urban cottage farmers fell into two types, settling on the land either alone or in small groups. Some aimed at commercial viability; others simply to break even and enjoy life. Most could rely on nothing beyond their own efforts. Like the communes, they attracted visitors, especially in the summer, who came to see how it was done and share, temporarily, in the rustic dream.

One of the earliest cottage farm settlements, the Methwold Fruit Farm Colony in Norfolk, was founded in 1889-90 by Mr R. K. Goodrich, who formerly ran a small business in London and who within ten years had fifty neighbours on two- and three-acre plots similar to his own. In 1893 he was visited by Herbert Rix of the New Fellowship and in 1899 by A. C. Sambrook, editor of the *Cable*, a magazine for the farming community founded by Lord Winchilsea. This account of the Methwold Fruit Farm Colony is taken from their words.

Mr Goodrich had planned his escape carefully: 'For three or four years he spent his evenings studying books on the land and the various occupations, such as fruit farming, poultry and bee-keeping, connected with it ... It looked so feasible that he began to think he would like to try it himself. His scheme was to colonise a small estate, to bring all possible skill and industry to bear on its cultivation and to sell the produce direct to the consumer.' Eventually he took the plunge: 'I decided to leave London and put it to the test. Just at that time the lease of my place in the City expired.' He bought a two-acre field at Methwold. 'The first thing to be done was to build a house. I drew the plans of my villa at Hornsey, the arrangements of which suited us very well, and built it myself. That is to say, I did not employ a contractor but the villagers of Methwold built it under my supervision. Then I planted about half the ground with fruit trees, made poultry runs and laid the remainder for vegetables. I had a good connection of friends in the City and obtained orders from them to take all the produce I could spare. And so the colony was started.'

Once established, Goodrich wrote to several newspapers describing what he had done, and 'it was not long before shoals of letters came from people who were anxious to give up their life in the towns and settle on smallholdings in the country ... Some of those who wrote to me paid a visit to Methwold and decided to come. Some have found that is was not exactly what they liked. A few have gone away. But the majority are still here.' The thirteen new plots were carved out of an adjacent field, each colonist paying £70 for two acres. Later other fields were subdivided in this way for new groups of settlers. Each plot was individually owned; as Goodrich was at pains to point out, he was no capitalist, buying up land to lease to others. He had no private means and his family was thus wholly dependent on their produce. 'There is no margin for luxuries, you may be sure,' he told Sambrook. 'We live simply and work hard but we are well and happy.'

Jan Marsh, *Back To The Land*, 1982

Tractorman

They said: Leave the city behind,
take strength from your roots.
Pausing from the drive, eyes turn
fieldwards – a tractor turning
winter into spring. I see him
everywhere these days, that
sack draped shape bent at the wheel.
Pausing at the field edge he
eases in the shares to wound the loam.
What shards may light in his furrows
he does not care to know. History
is a date picked out on the brick
of a school whose fallen beams bear
the chaff of harvests past;
the only pots are pint and pau.
I call, but words hardly cross
the space between us. My calls,
loud and long, cause pallor.
Have you seen a ghost, they ask?
I poke among the tangled growths broken
by the plough. Succour does not
grow well beneath these skies.
It is meet that in a time made
so much of circles I will return.
Through autumn's burning, hard fields
of winter, spring sowing and
summer reaping I proffer echoes
to this figure I see but cannot be.
I see him everywhere these days.

Paul Berry, *Earth Musk and Country Dark*, 1985

Pitchfork arts

Next day we had to get all the sheaves lifted out of the stooks and put into a stack. After that, when all the stacks were up we'd take a threshing machine up there to separate the barley grains out of each stack and leave the straw. Every sheaf had to be handled four times – up from behind the binder into the stook, from the stook on to the cart, from the cart to the stack, and then from the stack into the threshing machine. There was plenty of work on the farms at that time of year, as you can see, and that all depended on good weather to do it in. It was no good stacking or threshing wet corn. We didn't get to work on the field till midday when the dew had dried off a bit so we could start stackin' the shooves.

All this was done with a pitchfork, a long pole with two sharp prongs on the end, about a hand's breadth apart. They were polished and shone, and the long handle was made of ash. A sheaf of barley was about three foot long and weighed about a stone. That was thick and stalky at the butt end, and shaggy at the top or grain end. You had to be able to pick up a sheaf so that it balanced on the end of your pitchfork. You should then be able to swing it up so that that fell on the cartload more or less in place: someone stood in the cart to pack the sheaves, butts outwards, all round the cart. As you built the load, the thicker butt ends had to be round the edges of the cart, because they were bulkier than the heads so that the loads sloped inwards to the centre. This should make it stable, as the cart lumbered over the rough stubble ground. The load would sway from side to side anyway, but if the butts were outwards the load would tend to slip to the middle. If the load was built badly it would topple over and all the sheaves would have to be picked up again. And every time the sheaves fell about, some grain would be lost, knocked out of the head – that would be 'shed'.

Then, when the load of corn reached the stack, all the sheaves had to be lifted and placed again, in the same way. As the stack got higher, we'd use an elevator, with a little put-put motor, to take the sheaves up a blue thing, like a mechanical ladder, to the top. The corn had to be just right for the stack – not too wet or it would heat up. The farm workers would test a stack by thrusting an iron bar through it. If the stack had overheated, the iron got too hot to hold. If it was too hot when it was pulled out the whole stack would have to be quickly dismantled and, if the worst happened, all the straw would be going mouldy and bad, even black, and of course the grain in the head would be spoiled.

There was a lot to mind about when you used a pitchfork. You had to be careful you didn't stick that in anyone's face or into his thigh or into your foot, or other people's feet. If you used that clumsily, you could break up a sheaf and the straw would go every -where. Old Charlie Bacon could kill rats with his, spearing them like cheese on a toasting fork. It gave you a good feeling when you got a sheaf balanced right on your fork and you had the swing of it. The heavy bundle of barley seemed to fly up in the air and land exactly where you wanted it. But if you tried to lift a sheaf that was lying under another sheaf, or if you tried to lift the one you were standing on, Lord, that would give you gyp: you could really hurt your insides heaving at the tightly packed straw when nothing would move.

David Holbrook, *Getting It Wrong With Uncle Tom*, 1998

Smacks on the move

Gorleston played an important role in the Yarmouth herring fishing industry in the second part of the 19th century. The Short Blue Fleet, of over 220 fishing smacks owned by the Hewitt family and based at Barking on the Thames, moved part of their business to Gorleston in 1865. The spread of the railways and the need to find new fishing grounds were the main reasons for the move. The firm built their own shipyard, dry dock and ice house on a four acre site at the foot of what became known as Ice House Hill. Tunnels leading into the hill were used for storing salt, ice and tar, and a hostel was built for the smack boys next to Captain Manby's house in High Road. Cottages for the workers and their families, known as Hewitts buildings, were built off the High Street, Hewitt's Score leading from High Street to the company wharf. The cottage hospital in Trafalgar Road was largely paid for by the company.

The business had originated in 1764 and the name was taken from the square blue flag flown on all the company smacks. By the end of the century the majority of the fleet had moved from Barking to Gorleston and the company had become one of the town's main employers. In 1889 the building known as the Tower in High Street was built for Harvey George, company manager, and from here the fleet could be seen returning to port and prior arrangements made for berthing and unloading. Sail was giving way to steam and by 1901 the company had closed its original Thames base and concentrated on Gorleston, but by 1905 its operations had become seriously affected by steam trawling and it had started to reduce its fleet and dispose of its Gorleston property. The subsequent withdrawal of the Hewitt Fleet had a serious impact on Gorleston, almost 4,000 people having relied upon it for work and housing. Two public houses, the Barking Fishery and the Short Blue, were later named after the company.

Colin Tooke, *Gorleston and Southtown – At The Mouth Of The Yare*, 1994

Sugar beet

I became a farm hand next and found myself back in the Middle Ages gathering with other farm hands in front of the farmer first thing in the early morning, 6.30, to be informed of the day's tasks. I shared sugar-beet fields with a couple of other old hands, and I mean old, who shamed me by the speed they could move along rows of beet which had been churned into view by a machine ahead of us, and stayed bent lifting two beet, knocking them together to displace the earth, putting one down, with a sharp knife slicing the end of the other, flipping it in the air, catching it to slice the other end, dropping it, picking up the second beet, slicing that, dropping it, lifting another two - knock, top and tail, knock, top and tail. They left me standing in pain. I wrote a story about it – 'Sugar Beet' – which

I thought lyrical, capturing the expansive landscape, my misery, the dry mocking humour, the craggy personalities of the farm labourers, and the gorgeous Norfolk dialect with which I fell in love and was to use in four plays.

'Remember thaat Lond'ner what werked here last yier?'

'Thaat were 'afore my time wer'n it?'

'When d'yew come thin?'

'March o' this yier.'

'Just 'afore yow time thin. He were here three months 'afore Chrissmas. Yeap. he don' stay no longer. He'd hed enough a'ter the first couple o'days on sugar beet.'

'Yeap?'

'Yeap. He done say to owd Buckley, 'This ent noo test fer manhood, this is a test fer insanity!' An' owd Buckley he say to this chap, 'Yer better paack up thin.' An' he say, 'Yeap, I'd better.' He din laast long! Queer bor he were. He say ter me, 'Don' they hev machines ter dew this job?' An' I tell him they hev machines alright but it won' dew fer Buckley ter hev iny 'cos he won' waan us thin.'

'Noo, he won', thass trew 'nough. Hev a machine for the beet an' Buckley won' hev us go a'ter it in the winter. He'll send us a'ter the barley an' thaat'll be the lot fer us fer the yier.'

'I towld him thaat.'

'Whaat'd he say thin?'

'Huh! He don' say narthin', he just pull a face and carry on a'ter the beet an I ask him if when he git home he's gonna do iny gardnin'!'

'An' what'd he say to thaat?'

'He don't think thass funny 'cos he say, 'We ent got a garden!'.'

Arnold Wesker, *As Much As I Dare*, 1994

The Hovelleers

The dawn is breaking fiercely, it's been rough through the night,
The watchers on the cliff-top see a lame goose heave in sight.
Not a stitch of canvas on her, they can see by how she steers
That she's in dire trouble; call out the hovelleers.

   See her go a'marchin' with her great ole lugs'l set,
   Twenty bags to wind'd, lee gunnel slushin' wet,
   There's a hovel in the offin', but none need have no fears.
   For there goes the Norfolk hoveller, and her gallant
hovelleers.

They've got her to the water, see now how they row,
They're waiting for a level; look, there's the level now,
See them oars strike water, watch them pull her clear,
Each man's a splendid rower, for each man's a hovelleer.

   See her go a'marchin' ...

There's a prize there for the taking, not a stitch this goose can
set
And though they're tired and hungry, and their arses soakin'
wet
They'll get this ship to harbour, and then dole out their share,
One share for the hoveller, one each for the hovelleers.

   See her go a'marchin' ...

They'll take a pint o' porter and then make sail for home
Forty leagues or more boys, across the North Sea foam,
Their women will be waiting, but none will shed no tears
For they're Norfolk women and their men are hovelleers.

   O see her go a'marchin'...

Henry 'Shrimp' Davies, *Crabs and Shannocks*, 1983

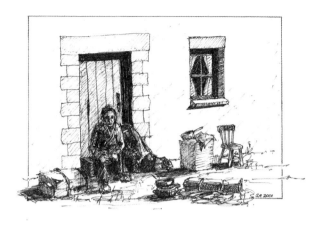

HARD TIMES

Norfolk's darker days are dominated by plague, persecution, fear of invasion and the unyielding privations of grinding poverty. The Black Death swept in from Europe to decimate 14th century Norwich and Yarmouth, and its long-term consequences sent tremors through hundreds of years. Jews and Quakers were among minorities who were to suffer in disturbing chapters of Norwich history. Napoleon's army, the Kaiser's threat and Hitler's power-crazy campaign all had the county bracing itself for possible incursions.

For all these massive concerns, it is the grim shadow of the workhouse and sheer misery of poverty, commonplace and seemingly incurable, that stands out starkly in so much local literature, fact and fiction.

Radical William Cobbett, who praised Norfolk and its people to the hilt in 1821 when he paid a call on his celebrated Rural Rides, had this harsh indictment of the countryside as a whole only a decade later: 'For my part, I am really ashamed to ride a fat horse, to have a full belly and to have a clean shirt on my back, while I look at these wretched countrymen of mine, while I see them actually reeling with weakness, when I see their poor faces nothing but skin and bone, while they are toiling to get the wheat and the meat ready to be carted away to be devoured by the tax-eaters.'

Maladies lingered on well into the 20th century until 'hard times' symbolised by the dreaded workhouse, became more a matter of bitter memory than bleak reality.

Workhouse Misery

It was in the year 1855 when I had my first experience of real distress. On my father's return home from work one night he was stopped by a policeman who searched his bag and took from it five turnips, which he was taking home to make his children an evening meal. There was no bread in the house. His wife and children were waiting for him to come home, but he was not allowed to do so.

He was arrested, taken before the magistrates next day, and committed to prison for fourteen days' hard labour for the crime of attempting to feed his children! The experience of that night I shall never forget.

The next morning we were taken into the workhouse, where we were kept all the winter. Although only five years old, I was not allowed to be with my mother.

On my father's release from prison he, of course, had also to come into the workhouse. Being branded as a thief, no farmer would employ him. But was he a thief? I say no, and a thousand times no! A nation that would not allow my father sufficient income to feed his children was responsible for any breach of the law he might have committed.

In the spring my father took us all out of the workhouse and we went back to our home. My father obtained work at brickmaking in the little village of Alby, about seven miles from Marsham. He was away from home all the week, and the pay for his work was 4s. per thousand bricks made, and he had to turn the clay with which the bricks were made three times. He was, however, by the assistance of one of my brothers, able to bring home to my mother about 13s. per week, which appeared almost a godsend. In the villages during the war hand-loom weaving was brought to a standstill, and thus my mother was unable to add to the family income by her own industry.

On coming out of the workhouse in March 1856 I secured my first job. It consisted of scaring crows from the fields of a farmer close to the house. I was then six years of age, and I was paid 1s. for a seven-day week. My first pay-day made me feel as proud as a duke. On receiving my wage I hastened home, made straight for my mother and gave her the whole shilling.

To her I said: 'Mother, this is my money. Now, we shall not want bread any more, and you will not have to cry again. You shall always have my money. I will always look after you.'

George Edwards, *Crow-Scaring to Westminster*, 1922

An Agricultural Ditty (1848)

Labourer
What art thou,
A beast, or a man?
Day work, or
Taken work
Live if thou can.

A beast, yes,
Is fed well,
He's kept in flash trim;
But this man
Who's rational
Just look at him.

Shadowy,
Skin-and-bone,
Bent down by his toil,
Hard-earned
Nine shillings,
Six days in the soil.

Carolus, in *East Anglian Verse*, Goodwyn, E. A., and Baxter, J. C. (eds), 1974

Black Death

The outbreak of plague in Norfolk in 1349, known at the time as the Great Pestilence and only later as the Black Death, was the main medical event of the Middle Ages in Norfolk, as it was throughout Europe. Exact figures of its mortality are difficult to ascertain but it is estimated that in the two Norfolk towns most severely affected, Great Yarmouth lost more than half its population and Norwich about two fifths of its then population of some 6,000 people. Mortality was also high in the villages and was particularly so among the clergy of the Diocese of whom 60% are said to have died. The medical profession was virtually helpless in advising on preventive measures or treatment and the ministrations of the clergy may account for their high mortality rate. The consequences of the Black Death were the first major example in Norfolk of the effects of a disease upon its social and economic life and scarcely any aspect of life was unaffected. It took a generation for Norwich and Norfolk to recover and the long term effects persisted over ensuing centuries.

Among the subsidiary consequences of the Black Death was the foundation of Trinity Hall, Cambridge, by William Bateman, Bishop of Norwich 1344-55, to train clerics to replace those who had died. A second was the view, still prevalent, that the Black Death is responsible for the isolated medieval churches, often some distance from human habitation, that adorn the Norfolk countryside. It was, however, only one of a number of factors that led to the depopulation or desertion of Norfolk villages. Even before 1349 some villages were in the process of being given up and it now seems certain that the Black Death was less responsible for Norfolk village depopulation than the replacement of people by sheep, introduced to supply wool to the booming cloth industry. A third legacy may be observed in some of Norfolk's medieval buildings. The main exporting port for north Norfolk's sheep country in the fourteenth century was Cley-next-the-Sea and its great church of St Margaret reflects the port's prosperity. Here the disparity between its magnificent nave and smaller chancel as well as some other architectural features are attributed to the Black Death; also the failure to erect a projected great west tower. Another example may be seen at Norwich Cathedral where the style of building of the east, south and west walks of the cloister is fourteenth century Decorated; in the north walk, mainly built after 1430, the style is Perpendicular. The long break between the building of the walks is again attributed to the Black Death.

Anthony Batty Shaw, *Norfolk and Norwich Medicine*, 1992

The cockle women

In a cosy vale is the village of Stiffkey. It is a curious little village noted for its cockle women. I went down to the long sea marsh. I crossed rotting timbers flung across creeks, and I went on for miles through mud and marsh till I came at length to the distant ridge of sand which has wrecked more ships than the Needles, and the incredible expanse of shore. Dotted about this gold plain were bent black figures raking up the famous 'Stewkey blues', as the cockles are called.

One cockle gatherer came towards me bent beneath the weight of an enormous sack. It was impossible to tell whether this strange figure was that of man or woman. She was wearing a black divided skirt. Thick worsted stockings, wet through with salt water, clung to her legs. She wore a black shawl over her shoulders and a sou'wester that buttoned like a Kate Greenaway bonnet beneath her chin. When I stopped her she lifted her face, and I saw that she was an ancient dame of at least seventy. Her toothless little mouth was pressed primly in below a smooth apple face etched with a million fine lines, and her eyes were blue and childish.

Like many people in this part of England, she was frightened of questions. I asked her if she was strong enough to do such hard work, and she said that she had been doing it since she was a young woman.

A few years ago some one wrote up Stiffkey and its cockle women in a cruel light. It was alleged that intermarriage had so affected the inhabitants that the men did not work while the women slaved to keep things going.

'That's a pack of nonsense,' said the ancient cockle gatherer. 'Our men work on the land, and we women have long before living memory gone down to the sea to get the cockles. I started when I was married, when I wanted extra money to bring up the children; and that's why most of us do it.'

She turned toward the sea and said:

'Those are the last cockle gatherers you'll see in Stiffkey. Girls today want to be ladies. They don't like to get themselves up in such ugly clothes and go down to the sea as their mothers and their grandmothers and – yes – and their great-grandmothers did; and they don't like hard work, either ... Yes, we're the last cockle women, we old ones ...'

A look of absolute horror came into the face of this old woman when I asked her if I might take a photograph of her. She put her hands to her eyes as I have seen Arabs do when faced by a camera.

'No, no,' she said, and looked around for cover. I soothed her with great difficulty.

It was not modesty, I think, or the thought of being photographed in such queer garments. Here and there in remote parts of England there exists still a curious belief that to be photographed brings bad luck.

There are few stranger sights in England than the return of these cockle women before the galloping tide. Slowly, heavily, they come with the great dripping sacks of 'Stewkey blues' on their backs. Most are old women, who belong to a tougher generation. Some are middle-aged. Now and again a girl goes down 'for fun', to see how her mother earned extra money to bring her up. The salt spray drenches their short skirts, the wind lashes their bare legs, as they come plodding in over the salt marshes.

This is a curious part of the world. A region barely touched by tourists. A region rich in history and packed full of atmosphere. You can stand on the salt marshes towards the end of the day, with the sun mellow over the windy fields of sea lavender, and it takes little to imagine the Viking ships beaching on the distant strand – the big, red-bearded men wading to the shore, dragging their great double-bladed swords through the purple marshes, shading their eyes to the distant land.

There is a melancholy over the sea marshes quite impossible to describe. You feel that it is good to be alone here, good to wander over the featureless land, listening to the shrill crying of the birds and to the sound of the wind in the grass.

H.V. Morton, *In Search of England*, 1927

The village – Norfolk 1830

The bitter year turned, the Assizes drew near, and the boy returned in the green twilight from bird-scaring in the field, through the village that had always been his home – his home quite as much as the four walls of the cottage where his father's empty chair stood like a mourner. In thatch and shutter, in woodsmoke mounting to the crystalline sky, in the figure of the hedger trudging down the sloping street beneath a great bundle of faggots like some prodigious hedgehog, in the geese squabbling about the half-frozen yard pond, in the skeleton of a wagon in the wheelwright's yard, in the old rooks' nests hanging like weird wintry fruit in the high trees around the church – in all these things there was such an intimacy that they might have been twined in the very fibres of the boy's heart. All how familiar, how true, how loved deep in the bones of him, yet how changed since the riot! Hard times there had been before, bitterness, gaunt resentment like harsh shapes beneath the snow, but still the village had never been less dear to him than the contours of his parents' faces seen in the chimney corner when the door was fastened against the night. Blighted now, blighted since that night and day when bitterness had flared and been snuffed out.

T. R. Wilson, *Heartsease*, 1993

Ben the Loafer

The look of the man I tremble to describe, but such an apparition as he presented to me one day as I came upon him threshing alone in a rickety little barn, with the thing he called his coat thrown into a corner, and his big brawny frame drawn up to its full height, I shall not soon forget. Caliban and Frankenstein's man *plus* something else very much of the earth earthy, were there combined in the strange figure that paused for a moment, stared, nodded, and then wielded the swinging flail as if the very grains of wheat would be pounded to dust under his mighty blows.

The first time I had an opportunity of talking to him, I had heard much less of Ben's ways than I have since learnt, and I am ashamed to think how good a chance I lost. His old parents were fading out of life, the vital spark in the mere ashes that remained gleaming every now and then, and twinkling, when the human dust was stirred by a basin of broth or a drop of some stimulant. They were feebly cowering over the shadow of a fire in the miserable shanty, and as I sat with them and felt my way to speaking of 'such things as pass human understanding', I fancied I saw the semblance of faint emotion in one or the other. Somehow I found myself kneeling down upon the mud floor.

Augustus Jessopp, *Arcady: For Better For Worse*, 1887

Petition to Sir Ed. Astley, Bart. and Wenman Coke, Esq., Knights of the Shire for the County of Norfolk

We the Little people of the hundreds of MITFORD and LAUNDITCH in your county ...
... In this struggle it is easy to foresee who must submit: for you know, and we know, the weakest must go by the walls. But we do implore you to speak for us in parliament, where we cannot speak for yourselves: and to stop as you easily can, that imprisonment of our persons, that separation from our children, that destruction of our race, that loss to The Kingdom, and that curse from The Almighty which must attend establishing a poor house upon the spacious fallacy of providing for our comfort, but he breaking of our hearts. The last we have to say to you is, though few of us may have votes, yet all of us have voices: and, we hope in God, you will not sacrifice so many of your helpless friends, to the haughtiness and greediness of the rest
... Let us not then be driven from these places of our settlement to become runagates, and to strip so many estates of their livestock: nor let us find our neighbours more cruel to us than what is felt by black slaves and savages bought in a market: while our laws if religiously attended to and well

executed for our fellow subjects, either provide for their subsistence at home in their own parish, or allow the easy union of a few parishes together, with all the owners and appointments that can be wanted to enforce industry without preventing population: and to supply our necessities, without much grievance to our supporters: so that if we are not well managed, it is not our fault. And remember if you will not help us in this extremity the younger part of us must, and will avoid gaining settlements within the bounds of these two hundreds, and the old and impotent not able to make resistance must be dragged to this house of confinement and die. With which gloomy prospect of present and future mischief to ourselves and families, to both king and people, we subscribe ourselves in tears and humility

Your devoted and afflicted Fellow Creatures and Countrymen

J. Crowley and A. Reid, *The Poor Law in Norfolk 1700-1850*, 1983

From the heart

Sometimes overseers received heartrending letters, but we wonder if it did rend their hearts? Here is one from Norwich, dated September 30, 1829. Apparently Hannah Edwards thought she had a settlement in Holt, for she wrote thus to the overseer:

Sir,

I am sorry to inform you that my Husband Thomas Edwards have Left me and two Children, he Left me intent to of and sike after work, and when he gott to London he heard of a Ship going to America at New York, and he sent me word he was going to America in that Ship. Now, Sir, I and my two Children are Left to God and the wide World, for, Sir, he toke all the money that he could gitt a Long with him, he Never Left me one Shilling. Now, Sir, I and my Children are Left to your Mercy, and, Sir, if you do not send me Some Relief Next Week I must apply to the Corporation of Norwich .... and, Sir, I am Sorry to inform you that I am in the

Family way, and expect to be Confined some time the Next Month. So, Sir, you must think that I am Left very uncomfortable. But I hope, Sir, that you will be A Friend to me and my Children.

In the end, Hannah and her children entered the Holt workhouse.

Jane Hales and W. Bennett, *Looking At Norfolk*, 1971

Sons of toil

Twenty-five shillings a week for fifty hours was the general rate for farm workers in Norfolk at the beginning of the year 1923. Some farmers paid a shilling or two more, a few paid as much as 30s., and, of course, special grades like carters and shepherds got higher pay. An examination of family budgets past and present, and the changes in food prices, showed that 25s. was equal to a wage of 14s.7d. in pre-war days. In other words, it was below the wage got by the labourers in the days of Joseph Arch, who raised the rate to 15s.

Norfolk men working on the land were once more reduced to the barest existence, to a skimping, mean condition. Going round the villages the correspondent of the ultra-Tory *Morning Post* was moved to tell readers of that paper: 'It is impossible to write without emotion of the agricultural distress prevailing in Norfolk. With wages at twenty-five shillings a week, the labourer is worse off than he has been in the memory of living man. He has cut down all expenses to the minimum. Pleasure and harmless amusements have been utterly banished from his life, though Heaven knows his frivolities in the past were simple and inexpensive enough. The pleasant hour passed over a pint of beer at the local inn, the conviviality which was the one break in the monotony of the long day's toil, the singing of folk songs passed down orally from one generation to another, all these are things of the past, for there is no money even to pay for half a pint of mild ale …'

Reg Groves, *Sharpen the Sickle!*, 1981

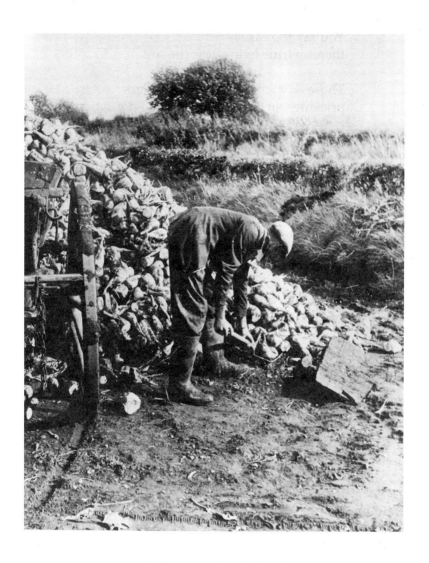

Loading sugar beet by hand

Celery Prickers

You say too easily
there's virtue living near the soil.

Those women crawling on all-fours
pricking-out celery plants would not agree.

For them there is no comfort in a cold east wind
whipping their broad behinds all day.

Even the canvas screen around each bed
cannot protect them from the black wet earth.

The only profit they get from the land
comes once a week to fatten each tight purse.

Watching them from the comfort of a car
you might compare their stitchery of plants

with that more gentle art of tapestry,
seeking some finery that is not there.

But stand outside and feel their bawdy talk
suck that glib thought from your unseasoned roots.

Edward Storey, *A Man in Winter*, 1972

Raid on city

In this first Baedeker raid on Norwich, 162 people died and
over 600 were injured. The *Eastern Daily Press* reported that
'all the defence services functioned admirably, and the dead
included many of their number ... Norwich has no reason to
be ashamed of herself, on the morning after the night before.'
The Regional Commissioner, Sir Will Spens, visited the city on
that morning to inspect the damage and to thank everyone
who had been involved in the night's work.

There were many accounts of that first raid, but nothing better illustrated the calm courage displayed by most Norwich citizens than a letter hurriedly penned by a reader of the *Eastern Daily Press* and published immediately afterwards. It read, in full:

> 1.30am, with our house intact, went across the city to my son and daughter-in-law. After a frantic half-hour among debris, by God's mercy found then safe and sound in nearby dugout. Then to our place of business; found it alight from end to end. To ease the mind of our managing director, again went across the city to enquire of his sister. Back to the business to tell him her house badly damaged, but the lady quite safe. Carry on at business, doing my puny bit. Asked to take message to total stranger: 'his son-in-law unable to return home last night, had to go out in the country'. Found the old gentleman gazing at a heap of bricks and mortar that a few hours back was 'four small tenements'. Delivered my message and received a fervent 'Thank you, my friend, we thought that he was under that lot!' Then, tired, filthy dirty, but humbly thankful, returned home and found everything the same as on any other morning - milk on the doorstep, letters and *Eastern Daily Press* on the mat. Messrs Milkmen, Postmen and Papermen, you are just or'nary people, but really you are rather wonderful.

After the first raid, mountains of rubble had to be shifted to rescue many who had been buried alive beneath it, and to recover the bodies of those who had been killed. Between 7 and 8 am pitiful queues of the bereaved and the destitute formed outside the City Hall. Loudspeaker vans toured the streets warning that water must be boiled, giving information about where various necessities could be obtained, and appealing to the able-bodied to remain at their posts.

R. Douglas Brown, *East Anglia 1942*, 1988

The Poor Widows Southrepps 1880

My mother, now aged ninety-seven, remembers that in the early 1880s a crude form of public assistance was carried on in a shed in the yard of the present butchers shop.

Very poor widows gathered there each week to receive one and sixpence in money and a small quantity of flour.

Sometimes a long wait in the wintry weather would have to be endured as the relieving officer (as he was known) came in a pony cart from Beckham. The poor old ladies all wore shawls.

Norfolk Federation of Women's Institutes, *Within Living Memory*, 1972

Breaking stones

What do these old fellows think about, I wonder, as they hobble to and fro round those measureless precincts of bald brick? The sweet-eyed children that they begot and bred up fifty years ago, perhaps, whose pet names they still remember, dead or lost to them today for the most part; or the bright waving cornfields whence they scared birds when they were lads from whom death and trouble were yet a long way off. I dare say, too, that deeper problems worry them at times in some dim half-apprehended fashion; at least I thought so when the other day I sat behind two of them in a church near the workhouse. They could not read, and I doubt if they understood much of what was passing, but I observed consideration in their eyes. Of what? Of the terror and the marvel of existence, perhaps, and of that good God whereof the parson is talking in those long unmeaning words. God! They know more of the devil and all his works; ill-paid labour, poverty, pain, and the infinite unrecorded tragedies of humble lives. God? They have never found Him. He must live beyond the workhouse wall – out there in the graveyard – in the waterlogged holes which very shortly –

Or perhaps their reflections are confined to memories of the untoothsome dinner of the yesterday and hopes of the meat pudding and tobacco to-morrow Who can tell? It would be useless to ask them.

At Heckingham there is a yard where tramps, in payment of their lodging, are set to break granite to be used in road repairs. To-day I had a try at this granite breaking, and a poor hand I made of the task. I hit hard and I hit softly, I hit with the grain and across it, I tried the large and the small hammer. As a result flakes of sharp stone flew up and struck me smartly in the face, but very little granite did I succeed in breaking. My companion tried also, and after him the master, who said that he understood the game, but neither of them did any better. I have come to the conclusion that even in breaking stones there must be a hidden art.

Henry Rider Haggard, *A Farmer's Year*, 1899

Enforced bath

What must have been the despair of many poor people on that May morning as they entered the workhouse for the first time and found themselves at once segregated according to the sacrosanct system of classification? The men were sent to one wing, the women to the other and children, unless infant at the breast, were separated from their parents in yet another wing. Many of these people had never even set foot in the village of Lingwood before and in those days of close parochial society, it would have been to them as though they were entering a hostile country. Then, the high white-washed walls, the tall windows, the smell of still-fresh plaster and disinfectant and black soap must have constituted a deep emotional shock, used as they were to the small, dark interior of their poor dwellings. The fact of finding themselves separated from their families in this building so much larger and more imposing than any they had ever seen would scarcely be alleviated by the presence of so many other persons, probably total strangers, with whom they were now thrown into forcible co-habitation. The cottage, the family unit had been the scale of their existence.

Then came the trauma of the enforced bath, the abandonment of the miserable but familiar clothes with which they had lived for so long, the donning of the new, stiff, uncomfortable workhouse garb, marked with the Union stamp and giving off an alien smell, the whole experience fraught by the distress of separation from spouse, children, parents, brothers and sister. The sense of shame at having had to come into the workhouse, the knowledge of having become a cipher instead of a person will surely have deepened as the days went by and workhouse discipline and time-table moulded them into inmates. Those first few meals, the luxury of that new bread delivered by Sarah Crowe of Acle can have done little towards alleviating the mental and emotional distress of many. The rigid discipline will have caused more than one rebellious spirit to rise.

Audrey Serreau, *Times and Years*, 2000

(1790) JULY 15, THURSDAY ... To a poor Woman from Dereham by name Hall with a small Child with her was taken very ill with a violent Pain within her by my great Gates and was laid down in the road, I went out to her and gave her a good Glass of Gin and gave her sixpence to go to the Inn, but she did not go there but returned back towards Dereham. She is a Widow and belongs to the House of Industry near Dereham. I hope she is no Impostor.

James Woodforde, *A Country Parson's Diary 1758–1802*

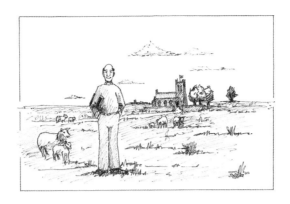

PEW AND PULPIT

All preachers great and small make up a fascinating collection in Church and Chapel – and Norfolk is particularly fortunate in the amount of written material left for future congregations. Lighting the way when it comes to proclaiming a proud parochial gospel are two clerics who moved to the county to continue their careers and happily found time to keep diaries.

Parson James Woodforde was born in Somerset and held a number of curacies before he was appointed in 1776 to the living at Weston Longville, a few miles from Norwich. He maintained a diary from the age of 18 until a few weeks before his death on New Year's Day in 1803. The Rev. Benjamin Armstrong was Vicar of East Dereham from 1850 until 1888.

Cyril Jolly, a pillar of Norfolk Methodism in the 20th century, plotted the movement's tempestuous beginning in this area as founder, John Wesley, and his itinerant preachers faced angry opposition. Cyril, himself a preacher and lover of the local dialect, also recorded the lighter side of chapel life … such as the time when hens wandered in during a service at Gressenhall.

There might have been a pecking order for local preachers on the circuit plan, but it is clear from many other observers that those who used simple and colourful Norfolk language often made the most impact. As one who sat through several eternity-length sermons in my old village chapel on glorious Sunday afternoons when there were cricket matches to watch, blackberries to pick and harvest fields to roam, I can vouch for the slight consolation of humour (much of it inadvertent) and a few sessions of pulpit banging!

First impressions

September 14th, 1850
Having this day been instituted by the Bishop of Norwich to the Vicarage of East Dereham, with the perpetual curacy of Hoe annexed, it becomes my duty to give some account of a place which, with God's blessing, is to be the scene of my future labours.

On the 13th I took the train from London to Norwich, the only objects of interest on the way being Cambridge in the distance, Ely Cathedral, and the breezy commons and plentiful game of Norfolk.

Ignoring the many thoughts which came crowding into my mind on beholding the first of these places, and passing by the flat fens of Cambridgeshire and part of Norfolk, let it suffice to transcribe, in this place, the following eulogy of Norfolk generally which I found in a directory at an inn. It is evidently from the pen of a Norfolk man, but, from general report, is not very far from the truth: 'Whether we survey this county with regard to its climate, population, commerce, the character of its inhabitants, its diversified beauties, or the improved state of its agriculture, it may with propriety be termed the glory of England'!

I was very favourably impressed with the City of Norwich; its numerous Gothic churches and quaint streets, its towering Castle and beautiful Cathedral, appeal to one powerfully; while its bustling activity and cheerfulness, its garrison and well-dressed inhabitants, quite take off the dullness which hangs over many cathedral cities. I though the Cathedral cramped, but this fault is atoned for by its antiquity, its Norman arches, and its entrancingly elegant spire. The service was tolerably performed by a thin choir, the boys being dressed in gowns of purple cloth. There was a fair congregation, and the Bishop was on his throne.

*   *   *   *   *

June 27th, 1866
My parishioners publicly presented me with a large cup and cover of chased silver, within which was a purple velvet purse

containing 100 guineas. The gift was accompanied by a list of the subscribers very beautifully illuminated and headed, 'Presented by the undermentioned subscribers to the Rev. B. J. Armstrong, with a cup containing 100 guineas, in recognition of the gratuitous establishment of a third Sunday service, and in testimony of their appreciation of his unremitting attention to his parochial duties during an incumbency of sixteen years. A.D. 1866.'

Considering that I came here in the year of the 'Papal Aggression,' when the public mind was highly irritated with the High Church party, I am astonished when, as I write, I see the silver goblet on the sideboard.

Rev. Benjamin Armstrong, *A Norfolk Diary*, 1876

Letters galore

Austin was habitually down first, and had usually polished off half his large correspondence before breakfast. People wrote to him about everything on earth. They solicited subscriptions for Poor Curates who must have been almost as well off as Barnham's poor Rector; they begged him to attend their village flower shows, lantern lectures, whist drives, sales of work; they asked him very frequently to take duty at their churches, knowing him to be the most amiable of men, who would put himself out to any extent to do a kindness; they asked advice on spiritual matters – women, these, to whom he replied briefly, 'Do as your conscience dictates; I cannot advise you, but can only pray that you may be well guided'; and more rarely, someone would write in an uneducated hand, either begging for money or complaining about the Relieving Officer: but as a rule the lower orders were reluctant to put labouring pen to paper, preferring to waste much more of the Rector's time in personal interviews.

Doreen Wallace, *Barnham Rectory*, 1934

Charges proved

Joseph Harrison, the vicar of Sustead in the 1630s, was brought before the Archbishop William Laud's High Commission, accused of being so drunk he could not read Divine Service. He was also said to have conducted secret marriages, secretly baptised illegitimate children, associated with beggars, tinkers and bedlam men, and been abusive to the Bishop of Lichfield. All these charges were proved and he was deprived of his living, fined fifty pounds, sent to prison and excommunicated. A further charge that he practised magic and charmed pigs did not succeed.

Thomas Hinde, *A Field Guide to the English Country Parson*, 1983

Cart-horse Preacher

It would have been no use
using the smooth liturgical words
of a cosy religion.
His congregation left their work
in the wet fields of the fen-country,
their cracked hands swollen
with beet-chopping.

To have asked them into the stiff pews
of a cold church would have meant
shouting at air; he knew
the hollow stillness of that place
left them more frozen than the fields,
and holy whining more than winter
lined their face.

So he gathered them round him
on the market square, saying
'I'll speak a language you can understand,
who cares about the lovely use of words
when half the words are nothing more than sound'.
  Their frost-blue ears were tingled
  by his fire.

They met him every Sunday-night and knew
God would be called a muck-heap
or a cow, and no irreverence meant.
'Crops thrive,' he'd say, 'where muck is spread,
and milk pumps life in every sucker's mouth'.
He solved the mystery of their fields,
healed their backs.

But now he's dead, and God's
locked in His church, stiff and alone.
Men work their days out on the land
wondering why the old cart-horse preacher
bothered them at all. Sometimes they feel
without him frost stays longer in their hands
and limbs more often ache.

Edward Storey, *North Bank Night*, 1969

The long service

The regular vicar was about to take his fortnight's holiday; so
he called to see his friend the rector of a nearby parish. 'Would
you kindly take the service for me in my church next Sunday?'
he asked. His friend readily consented and duly turned up at
the church at the appointed time. Old Isaac the dairy farmer,
was the only parishioner to turn up.

After waiting a while, the Rector said, 'Well, it says in the
good book, that when two, three or more are gathered together
– thou shalt grant their request. But this is ridiculous, here I
have a congregation of only one, do you think I should take
the service?'

'Look here, master,' said Isaac, 'when I take a load of hay
down to the bottom meadow to feed my herd and only one
turns up, I feed it.'

The rector thought, 'Well, it looks as if he wants me to take
the service,' which he did, for a full hour and a half.

'Was that all right?' he asked Isaac at the end.

'Look here master,' the old farmer replied. 'When I take that load of hay down to the bottom meadow, to feed my herd, and only one turns up. I don't give it the whole durn load!'

Frank Etheridge, *Salt on a White Plate*, 1989

A born teacher

Much might be written on the language indulged in by the local preachers, even at the present day, often bordering as it does on the ludicrous, but with all sincerity I grant.

One of these 'locals,' whom I shall call Sam, was very popular, no camp-meeting was considered a success without a few words from him, or one of his 'nanny-goats,' as the scoffers avowed he once slipped out for anecdotes. Sam was a veritable type of a country yokel, ruddy faced, ginger hair and beard. He stood six feet, owned a voice like that of the proverbial herald, and possessed enough muscular Christianity to thump the inside out of a pulpit Bible, or remove a noisy Philistine out of his congregation. His similes often dropped to the burlesque; but he was a born teacher, and his audience seldom failed to carry away the gist of his discourse. I remember him once taking for his text, 'The wages of sin is death.' Sam prefaced his sermon as follows: 'My frinds, brother Paul tells us that th'waages o' sin is death, Now let's see wuther we kin graasp wot he maan by't. S'pose I wor tu go an' du my haarwest for Mr. H– (a local farmer), an' arter all th' wuk wor dun, go an' ax Mr. T– (another farmer in the same village) fur my waages, wot du yeou think Mr. T– would saay? Sure-ly he would up and saay, 'Sam, yeou air a fule, go and ax Mr. H – fur yer waage, yeou ha' dun yer haarwest there, wot du yeou come an' ax me fur yer waages fur?' An' ef I wuk all my loife fur th' daavil an' go tu God fur my reward, He wool saay, 'No, no, Sam, yeou go tu th' daavil fur yer reward, yeou hev wuked fur him in the haarwest o' loife, he must pay yeou!''

Walton N. Dew, *A Dyshe of Norfolke Dumplings*, 1898

Sermon surprise

The building was once a barn, and the house to which it is attached may have been a farmhouse. It is not certain what denomination originally used it as a place of worship, but it seem likely that this use dates from the early nineteenth century.

The Gressenhall congregation belonged to several Methodist connexions until the 1932 amalgamation brought them into what is now the Methodist Church. In 1923 the building had been bought by the United Methodist Church, after a house-to-house collection had raised part of the money, and the owner had re-tiled the roof at his own expense. In Cyril Jolly's little book about God's Cottage there is a story of how a preacher from nearby North Elmham looked up from his sermon notes one warm summer afternoon to see three or four hens strut into the chapel. No one wanted to eject them, because of the commotion it might cause, so they were allowed to file with dignity to the front of the chapel, where 'after gazing about them and clucking in approval, they settled down until the service was over'.

John Hibbs, *The Country Chapel*, 1988

Parson's pain

June 4, 1776 … My tooth pained me all night, got up a little after 5 this morning, & sent for one Reeves a man who draws teeth in this parish, and about 7 he came and drew my tooth, but shockingly bad indeed, he broke away a great piece of my gum and broke one of the fangs of the tooth, it gave me exquisite pain all the day after, and my Face was swelled prodigiously in the evening and much pain. Very bad and in much pain the whole day long. Gave the old man that drew it however 0. 2. 6. He is too old, I think, to draw teeth, can't see very well.

June 4, 1776 … Very much disturbed in the night by our dog which was kept within doors tonight, was obliged to get out of bed naked twice or thrice to make him quiet, had him into my room, and there he emptied himself all over the room. Was obliged then to order him to be turned out with Bill did. My face much swelled but rather easier than yesterday tho' now very tender and painful, kept in today mostly.

James Woodforde, *A Country Parson's Diary 1758–1802*

Up and down

Dr Bowers was selected to preach at St Paul's Cathedral one Sunday morning. On his way up the numerous steps leading to the cathedral, he saw a dear old lady crawling up in rather crab-like fashion, and, being a 'perfect little gentleman', he offered his arm. When nearly at the top the old lady stopped to get her breath, and said, 'And can you tell me, sir, who is to preach to us this morning?' Dr Bowers, with a modest smile, answered, 'Yes, I can. It is the Bishop of Thetford,' to which the old lady replied, 'Oh dear! oh, dear! I don't like him at all. Will you please take me down again?'

B. Knyvet Wilson, *Norfolk Tales and Memories*, 1930

Late collection

It was the custom for preachers with cars to convey other preachers to their appointments and collect them on the way back. This village was the nearest to our town and consequently I was dropped off first and would be collected last . However, after I had pronounced the Blessing, one of the congregation stood up and began to pray, to be followed by another and then another until all twelve or so had contributed. Naturally, I became very concerned that all my colleagues must have been outside waiting for some considerable time by then and when I finally dashed out all apologetic, I found them sitting there with broad grins on their faces. They knew what would happen, but hadn't seen fit to warn me.

At a nearby chapel worshipped two brothers who had apparently not spoken for years. They would sit on opposite sides of the chapel and persistently avoid each other (and I've had tea with each on different occasions.) I was told that it was a harkback to when their mother had died and they couldn't agree who should have her chair! Happily, I understand that they finally made their peace.

Malcolm Rix, *Never Forget*, 1992

All creatures ...

On April 29th, 1898, the Vicar gave a Lecture in the School, which was somewhat of a novelty in Horning. The lecture was entitled 'Some wonders of the microscope', and was illustrated by a powerful lantern microscope, illuminated by the oxy-ether light, worked by Mr. E. H. Stevenson of Norwich. A mounted specimen of the common flea was first thrown on to the 7-ft screen, and increased from 15 inches up to 15 feet in length. Under the highest power only the head and legs could find room on the screen at one time. Several mounted transparent objects were shewn, including the blow-fly's tongue and the eye of a beetle, the thousands of lenses in the latter being plainly visible to all in the room. The greater part of the evening, however, was taken up with the exhibition of some twenty different species of live insects and other animals collected from dykes and ponds in the neighbourhood. These created much amusement by their lively antics on the screen. The palpitating heart of the water flea was very distinctly seen, as was all the internal anatomy of this curious little crustacean. The gymnastics of two gnat pupae caused immense merriment, and the complicated jaws of the larvae both of the gnat and the dragon-fly, were admirably displayed, as they were both kind enough to put their apparatus in motion for our benefit. (Proceeds after paying £1 – 5s expenses, 14s 10d for the Church Curtain fund.)

Susan Yaxley, *The Rector Will Be Glad*, 1992

Wesley's walk

The first record of Methodism in Hempnall is of James Wheatley, the Methodist preacher who had missioned Norwich in 1751, licensing 'the house of William Roberts and John Fuller in Hempnall,' on 15th January, 1754. Five years pass and John Wesley comes, not on a horse as we associate with him, nor by chaise or coach, but he walked the nine miles from Norwich. That was on 4th September, 1759, with harvest still in progress. At noon he took his stand under an oak tree where three roads met (the war memorial now stands upon the spot), and prepared to preach. The people knew of his coming and gathered to hear him, but opposition was ready, and the ringleader of a gang began blowing a horn, but someone who wanted to hear what the little man in clerical dress had to say, seized the horn, and the man and his companions, seeing the temper of the crowd was not in their favour, ceased their disturbance and Wesley addressed a 'deeply attentive people' on 'By Grace are ye saved through faith,' Ephesians II, 8.

The oak tree under which that sermon was preached became known as Wesley's Tree, until it was cut down to erect the war memorial. On 4th September, at noon, two hundred years later, Methodists gathered on the spot to commemorate Wesley's coming.

Such open-air preaching was not Wesley's choice; he said, 'The devil does not like field preaching. Neither do I. I love a commodious room, a soft cushion, a handsome pulpit. But where is my zeal if I do not trample all these under foot in order to save one more soul?'

Eleven years after Wesley's visit the parish register records the death of a young woman, Dorothy Pitts, and comments, 'A sober and well disposed young woman aged 17 who kept clear from the taint of Methodism.'

Cyril Jolly, *The Spreading Flame*, 1974

Sonorous boom

The grossness of his speech and action did not prevent him from being a zealous professor of Primitive Methodism. Every Sunday he attended nine o'clock service at the little stable of a chapel at Turlham. When a rest was given to local talent, and a strange 'preacher' came over in a hard felt hat and a tail coat, for a fee of ten shillings and his dinner, it was at Noddyfield's that his dinner was provided. On such occasions Philip, his wife Peggie, and their 'innocent' son Bertie had the honour of escorting the preacher to afternoon service, though as a general rule Peggie and Bertie patronised the church as being 'more serciety'. On Wednesday evenings the blind man was always in great force at the chapel, and had been heard to lift up his voice in extemporaneous prayer 'most bewtiful'. He was even frequently known to officiate as 'preacher,' and when it was anticipated that his sonorous boom would fill the chapel with unctuous self-righteousness and suave hypocrisy there was always a full congregation. The reason was that a preacher with eyes could exercise a certain supervision over the conduct of his audience. But when old Noddy held forth there was no one in an elevated position to see what the boys an girls of the village were doing. One who added to his powers of exhortation the blessing of sight might object to what he saw. But old Noddy couldn't see. Hence his popularity as an expounder of the Gospels.

James Blyth, *Juicy Joe*, 1903

Brotherly discipline

The Local Preachers' Meeting was very concerned about neglect of appointments. It was made a rule 'That the preachers who wilfully neglect their appointments, shall, for such neglect, sink one figure on the plan.' This may seem severe, but neglect of an appointment was repeatedly said to be the cause of membership decreases.

At the L. P. meeting in 1842 practically every Minute was of a disciplinary nature:-

1. One brother was removed from the plan for various reasons including that of 'going to America without informing his wife.'

2. One of the Travelling Preachers was reprimanded for boxing his son's ears too soundly.

3. A preacher was suspended for six months for 'wasting his time sitting in a public house.'

4. Four preachers did 'sink one place' and one sister 'two places.'

5. Another preacher was admonished for 'agitating the Bawdeswell society.'

Discipline also occupied the time of the Full Board. Bro. X had neglected his appointments and when his case was discussed it was felt that he was justified in staying from an appointment through having a sore foot, but he was reprimanded for neglecting another appointment because of rain.

Cyril Jolly, *History of the East Dereham Methodist Circuit*, 1955

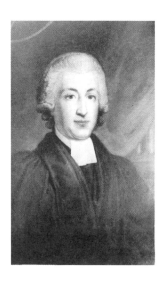

Parson James Woodforde

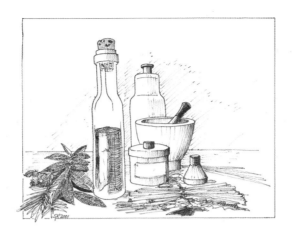

CURES AND REMEDIES

Despite the great advances of modern medicine, many old-fashioned remedies, handed down from generation to generation, are still in circulation. Indeed, country cures, complementary to orthodox medicine, continue to bring relief in some quarters.

When many of the remedies highlighted in this section were in common use, there were no alternatives, especially in remote rural areas where the doctor was inaccessible because of cost and distance.

Not that all suggestions ought to be taken too seriously. We have no living examples of toothache sufferers who filled their mouths with cold water and sat on the hob until the water boiled. And some of the 'cures' for whooping cough involving roasted or fried mice take some swallowing.

Still, it is a menu rich in folklore and intriguing stories. For example, early in the 1900s one of the Friendly Societies in a Norfolk village advised a member to get in touch with the local wise woman. The member had presented so many certificates from the doctor that the sick fund was in serious danger of exhaustion. It was thought that 'Old Mother Brown' and her age-old remedies should at least be tried.

Goose grease

My father was not only a vermin destroyer all his life, as his father and grandfather had been before him, but he also knew a great deal about herbs and plants which could be useful in curing sickness. As I was out with him so much in the Fens as he worked, he was able to point out to me where these herbs grew and how and for what they could be used; in this way he taught me most of what he knew, and even today I am often asked for some of these old remedies of his, and people find them most helpful.

We always kept part of the garden stocked with rosemary, thyme, horehound, rue, mint, sage, sorrel and many other herbs, and when we were out mole-catching we often found, especially on the old Wash bank, other plants which could be made up into medicines. In those days not many people could afford to go to the doctor, especially for ordinary, minor complaints, and as there was no National Health Service they had to find their own cures for nearly every illness.

Every spring my mother would make stinging-nettle tea and give us children two glasses of it every day. This was very good for nettle rash or prickly heat – it 'changed our blood' she used to say – but if we had any signs of scurvy between the fingers then she would add a handful of Hairweed to the nettles. The mixture was sweetened with sugar and, though it tasted rather sickly, it was not too unpleasant to drink.

To cure a very bad cold on the chest she would fold a sheet of dark brown paper and cut it so that, when it was opened out it formed the shape of a heart – this was most important. The paper was then covered with Russian tallow or goose grease, placed on the chest and kept there by means of a scarf. This soon eased the most troublesome cough and though it struck cold when it was first put on it soon warmed up and felt quite comfortable. Goose grease is excellent for easing any tightness in the chest or for a sore throat and is equally good when eaten on toast or bread.

Arthur Randell, *Sixty Years a Fenman*, 1966

Moles and molars

Some while ago I had been suffering from toothache, and met an old friend of mine in a Norfolk village. He inquired as to my health and at once said, 'Jaw-ache! Dew yew know what you ought to dew?' He said he had been out 'with a young feller' after a 'bit of sput' and some of the captures were moles (or 'molls' as he called them). On their way back they had 'happened across' another 'young feller' who was suffering from 'jaw-ache'. My old friend went on: 'Well, this hare young feller what went out along of me, say, 'I can cure him,' he say, and I said, 'What do yew mean?' and he say, 'Hev yew got any old molls in your bag?' and then he sorted 'em over and picked out a female moll. Then he took out his shet knife and took and cut the fore paws off this old moll and gan 'em to this hare young feller with the jaw-ache, and he say, 'Now yew take and keep them in your weskit pockut, and you'll never have another jaw-ache as long as you live' – and,' my friend concluded, 'he never did.' I expressed deep interest, and he then said. 'An' if you're a female and you git the jaw-ache, yew take and cut the paws off the male moll, yer see.' I then said I thought I had better see the dentist and he was very much hurt. 'Well, a-course, yew kin dew as yew like about that!'

B. Knyvet Wilson, *Norfolk Tales and Memories*, 1930

Expat advice

The story is told of a north Norfolk fisherman who came into his local pub looking drawn and miserable, with his hand bandaged. The publican asked him what had happened, and he explained that while gutting a fish he had got a bone buried in his hand, and he had been unable to remove it. The publican sent one of his customers out to the field behind the pub to fetch a large dock leaf and a cow pat. The fresh cow manure was plastered on the man's hand, which was then wrapped in the dock leaf. The patient complained of awful pain in his hand. 'Never mind, drink up', he was ordered, and a pint put in front of him. Some half an hour later, the poultice was removed, and there was the white end of the cod-bone sticking up. It was quite easily removed!

Fresh cow pats were quite commonly used in this way, for treating animals and humans. A Norfolk postmaster recalls his father curing a foal with a badly cut leg, using fresh cow dung and a potion which he made. The leg healed without a scar.

Gabrielle Hatfield, *Country Remedies*, 1994

Grandma's tips

Stomach trouble:
Swallow a live spider – stomach guaranteed to become thoroughly clean.

Anaemia:
Gather quantity of rusty iron nails, do not wash but boil for several hours, take half teacup of liquid, sweetened, three times a day.

For septic sore:
Rub on live snail or burnt alum to draw poison.

For bleeding or cuts:
Cover wound with cobweb or raw tobacco.

Dick Joice, *Full Circle*, 1991

Mother's shelf

Mother had a shelf in the kitchen cupboard for her remedies. There were small corked glass bottles containing oil of peppermint, oil of juniper and oil of eucalyptus. A few drops were served on a sugar lump, of peppermint for indigestion and of juniper for chills in our waterworks. The eucalyptus oil was rubbed into our chests to help a stuffy cold. We also had two popular drinks to relieve coughs and colds – blackcurrant tea, which was a spoonful of blackcurrant jam in a cup of hot water, and butter, vinegar and honey melted in a saucepan and sipped very hot. Catarrh was relieved by sniffing warm salt water.

Senna pods were soaked overnight and the resulting water was drunk the next morning to deal with constipation. Diarrhoea was stopped by spreading a thin layer of flour on a baking tin; this was baked in the oven until it turned a light golden brown, then mixed with water and drunk.

Norfolk Federation of Women's Institutes, *Within Living Memory*, 1995

Silver coins

EPILEPSY is cured, in the case of an unmarried woman, by begging from nine bachelors as many silver coins - generally threepenny-bits – these are made into a ring and worn by the sufferer on the fourth finger of the left hand. To cure a man, maidens must supply the needful. A ring made of a half-crown from the communion offertory, is also worn for the same purpose. The blood of a live mole dropped on a lump of sugar and taken, is good for fits.
For RHEUMATISM and NEURALGIA etc. Wear in the pocket the right foot of a female hare. Always dress and undress the left side first. An extracted tooth should be burnt, or 'a dog's tooth' may grow in its place. I have not admitted as canonical the remedy so often suggested to the sufferer with toothache, viz., fill the mouth with cold water and sit on the hob until the water boils, as there is no recorded instance of its being tried.

Walton N. Dew, *A Dyshe of Norfolk Dumplings*, 1898

Home and farm

For colds, a mangold had to be washed with the skin on, sliced, and placed on a big dish. Brown sugar was sprinkled on it, and then it had to stand and drain. A dessert-spoonful was recommended four times a day. This was a great help for whooping-cough. Chilblains were rubbed in mutton fat. Sulphur and treacle (or Epsom salts) once a week kept one's bowels right. A cut finger had to be washed and rubbed in salt. Try it. A ground dried acorn was the answer to diarrhoea when taken in hot milk. In winter feet were kept dry if mutton fat was rubbed well into one's boots.

On the farm, a cow which was off her food was given ivy. For a calf with diarrhoea, a whole egg had to be broken into its mouth so that it swallowed the lot. This was done twice a day. A sow that had just farrowed and was poorly was given a red herring. If a cow knocked a horn off, a good thick cobweb wound round would stop the bleeding. Some horsemen would collect from the vet. a special ball which they would give the horses once a week. The horse's mouth would be opened, and while its tongue was grabbed the ball would be pushed down its throat with the other hand, far enough to be swallowed. If you watched closely, you could see it go down.

Arthur Amis, *From Dawn to Dusk*, 1992

The good huswifelie

GOOD huswives provides, ere an sickness doo come,
   of sundrie good things in hir house to have some.
Good Aqua composita, Vineger tart,
   Rose water and treakle, to comfort the hart.

Cold herbes in hir garden for agues that burne,
   that over strong heat to good temper may turne,
While Endive and Suckerie, with Spinnage ynough,
   all such with good pot herbes should follow the plough.

Get water of Fumentorie, Liver to coole,
   and others the like, or els lie like a foole.
Conserve of the Barbarie, Quinces and such,
   with Sirops that easeth the sickly so much.

Aske *Medicus* counsell, ere medicine ye make,
    and honour that man, for necessities sake.
Though thousands hate physick, because of the cost,
    yet thousands it helpeth, that else should be lost.

Good broth and good keeping doo much now and than,
    good diet with wisedome best conforteth man.
In health to be stirring shall profit thee best,
    in sicknes hate trouble, seeke quiet and rest.

Remember thy soule, let no fansie prevaile,
    make readie to Godward, let faith never quaile.
The sooner thy selfe thou submittest to God,
    the sooner he ceaseth to scourge with his rod.

Thomas Tusser, *Five Hundred Points of Good Husbandry*, 1557

Henry's herbs

Letter from James, now back in the purlieus of W.12, to say
that Angela has another touch of sciatica, and have I any more
of those herbs, as they seemed to do the trick last time? So
pack up a selection from the young sheaf hanging from the
attic rafters, the while I recall the cheerful grin, the bright
succory-blue eyes, and the Father Christmas beard of Henry
Knights, pottering about in the wooden shed which housed a
car nearly as old as himself, and bundles of the herbs he
collected at appropriate seasons.

Many were the stories told of invalids who visited him for
the first time driven in a dog-cart or pony-trap, so 'set fast'
with rheumatism or lumbago that they had to be helped down
from their conveyances. Sent away with a bunch of dried
'harbes', plus instructions on how to use them, their next call
would be paid on foot, sometimes from a distance of several
miles. His remedy for both complaints was much the same.
Agrimony: a tall woody-stalked plant with a spike of small
yellow flowers; succory: another woody-stemmed plant with
blue flowers, which is also known as chicory, and wormwood,

were its chief ingredients. A good-sized bunch of the first two, with a dash of the third ... or succory or agrimony used alone ... to be thrust into a saucepan, partially covered with boiling water, then simmered from two to three hours. The resultant brew, in taste and texture not unlike strong, slightly bitter tea, to be taken in quantities roughly approximating two pints per week for three weeks (or longer should, by any chance, the condition persist). Henry Knights could toss off a day or two's ration at one gulp without apparent ill-effects, but the general rule was a wineglassful three times a day, preferably after meals.

Elizabeth Harland, *No Halt At Sunset*, 1951

Parson's plight

March 11th, 1791 : The Stiony on my right Eye-lid still swelled and inflamed very much. As it is commonly said that the Eye-lid being rubbed by the tail of a black Cat would do it much good if not entirely cure it, and having a black Cat, a little before dinner I made a trial of it, and very soon after dinner I found my Eye-lid much abated of the swelling and almost free from Pain. I cannot therefore but conclude it to be of the greatest service to a Stiony on the Eye-lid. Any other Cats Tail may have the above effect in all probability, but I did my Eye-lid with my own black Tom Cat's tail.

James Woodforde, *A Country Parson's Diary 1758–1802*

Betty's gifts

I will not try my reader's credulity by describing in detail the particular manifestations which at once and for ever rent the veil between Betty and the higher intelligences about her, and made her conversant with the language of the unseen world. Without the conviction and sincerity of the old lady's voice, and the serene truth engraved in every wrinkle of her sweet old face, in every line of the noble features, and beaming from the depth of her kind eyes, such a description would be as bizarre and incredible as an Arabian tale of Jinns and Afrites to the age which has discovered protoplasm, and lost its sight in gazing at that wonder.

From this time forth Betty began to bring comfort to many in trouble, and health to many in sickness. The herbs and roots of marsh, meadow, and woodland became a magical pharmacopoeia to her. Marshmallow and crowfoot, dandelion and sorrel, rue and penny royal, deadly nightshade and henbane, juniper and broom, yielded their secrets to her broths and teas. Even if the title of 'white witch' be an anachronism not to be allowed in civilised communities, Betty's gifts as a herbalist were sufficient in Frogsthorpe to raise a prima facie presumption in favour of her possession of supernatural powers.

James Blyth, *Juicy Joe*, 1903

Healing warts

There are many persons who profess to cure warts, or 'writs,' as they are sometimes called, by passing the hand over them and muttering at the same time some mysterious word. If persons have any scruple about consulting such accredited professors of the healing art, they may get rid of their warts in other ways. Thus, let the patient steal a piece of beef (it must be stolen or it will have no efficacy), and bury it in the ground, and then as the beef decays the warts will gradually die away. Or make the sign of the cross on each wart with a pin or pebble stone, and then throw the pin or pebble away. Or go to an ash tree which has its 'keys,' that is, husks with seeds, upon it, and cut the initial letter both of your Christian and surname on the bark. It is then necessary to count the exact number of the warts, and, in addition to the letters, to cut a notch for each. The result will be that as the bark grows up the warts will go away. Or take the froth of new beer and apply it on three successive mornings to the warts, when no one can see you. The froth must not be wiped away, but allowed to work off of itself, and then the warts will disappear. Or gather a green sloe, rub it on your warts, throw it over your left shoulder, and you will soon be free from them. I have been told of a boy thirteen years old who had a large number of 'writs' on his hands. He attended school, and one Friday the schoolmaster, who had frequently seen the boy's hands dirty from the number of 'writs', asked him to count them accurately, and then tell him the exact number. The lad did so, and some days afterwards he was startled by the boy who sat next to him at the desk exclaiming, 'Why, Tom, where are your writs?' They were all gone.

John Glyde Jnr., *Folklore and Customs of Norfolk*, 1872

Village medicine

May 14th, 1956

Deer Sar – Thank yow fer yar kind wishes. I'm a gitten on, but I aren't right, not yit. I shull heter keen a duen...

Our Doctor, he's a fine man, he meark yer fear better, if he only come an see yer, an thas afore he gi' yer any medesen.

Now he told my Aunt Agatha this. (He think tha world o' har. She often help him with ould peeple wot arnt well.) Of course Doctor git fed up wi' these here wimen what go ter his sargery, when in most cearses there earnnt really northen tha' matter with 'em.

Well, one mornen Doctor looked inter his waiten rume, an there they set, seven wimen (all his 'reglars'), an one man.

He sed to 'em all, 'Now this mornen I'm a'gorne to give you all a thorough examineartion an see wot really is tha' matter, wi' tha' hull lot on yer. I'll teark this gentleman first, an yow leardies can be a unloosernen, and gitten fit.'

Well, oul Mrs. W— an har pal shot out right away. Mrs. W— say, 'I dint come here prepared fer no examineartion, neither wi' mi' clothes, an yit me' feet.' Har pal say, 'More dint I.'

Well, that feller hearnt bin in that sargery many minutes afore he gan such a yell. He hallered out, 'Oh Doctor, you're a haatten me, you're a killen me.' You could a herd him down ter tha Crown.

Well, four o' them wimen shot outer that waiten rume an

never stopped 'till they got unter tha high rood, then they started a duen up what they started unduen.

When Doctor looked inter his waiten rume, there set just one oul leardy, bolt upright, a holden her medesen bottle. That tarned out, she was stone deaf. Of corse that man what the Doctor called in first, wuss a pal of his, that wuss a put up jorb. Anyhow that worked all right, becos tha Doctor ha' hed werry few 'reglars' leartly.

Well, once agin, fare-yer-well, tergather. - Yars obediently,
THE BOY JOHN.

Sidney Grapes, 'The Boy John Letters', *Eastern Daily Press*, 1956

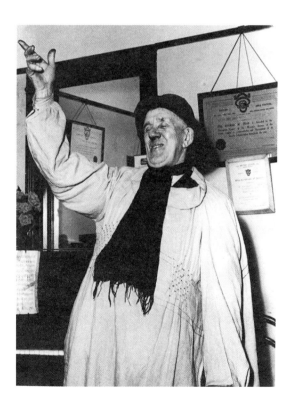

Sidney Grapes – The Boy John

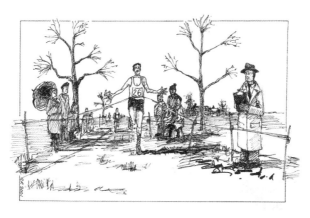

SPORTING CHANCE

As a sporting journalist throughout the 1970s, specialising in covering the fortunes and otherwise of Norwich City Football Club for the local press, I had little trouble finding candidates for this collection. Indeed, I needed to be ruthless not to concentrate solely on that decade which saw the Canaries soar to soccer's top flight and flutter at Wembley for the first time. Even so, two of my valued colleagues during those heady days, sports editor Ted Bell, and fellow Carrow Road scribe Bruce Robinson, earned places on this local sporting podium.

My love of cricket, surviving the commercial juggernaut that is flattening so many old-fashioned virtues, finds full expression in the unofficial Test Match at Old Buckenham in 1921 when Jack Hobbs played one of the finest innings of his marvellous career.

Inevitably, there are soccer salutes for the cup-fighting Canaries of 1958-59, but it was much more a case of black and blue rather than yellow and green when the ancient game of camp-ball, or camping, held sway. Athletic feats and amusing punchlines from Les King, one of the county's most colourful sporting characters of recent times, are also included on this little roll of honour.

And another old friend and colleague on the Eastern Daily Press, *the redoubtable Jonathan Mardle, provides a perfect reminder of how he could turn his pen to any subject under the Norfolk sun with a memorable portrait of Barton Regatta on August Bank Holiday.*

Boxing lessons

One day when my dad was working at the Deopham Green airbase, an American kindly gave him two pairs of boxing gloves, which he brought home and gave to me. Two houses away lived another lad called Geoffrey Buckenham, who was older and heavier than me. He came round our back yard and we were soon sparring, but he knocked me about a bit and I came off the worse for wear. I could only improve.

I was about ten or twelve years old and needed to be taught how to box. There were some people living in Hingham, who knew something about the sport, and I decided to go and see them.

My first call was at Pig's Hill, where I visited a man called Pop Lane, who also worked at the airbase as a storeman. He had shown several Americans how to box and he taught me to use my left as well as how to hold my hands to defend myself. When I left, Pop said to me, 'It will be a long time, son, before you are another Joe Louis.'

At that time, living down the Folly, was an ex-navy boxing champion, whose name was Harry Toerags Eke. When I called to see him with my boxing gloves, he reminded me of Popeye. He had a grey beard and smoked his pipe upside down. As I biked into his yard he shouted, 'What do you want, boy?' I replied that I wanted some boxing lessons and he smiled saying, 'Put them there gloves on.' He gave me some instructions and, as he sparred with me, he still had his pipe in his mouth upside down, but I still could not hit him.

My boxing lessons continued, but it was not long before I had the chance to see if I had learnt anything. On Sunday nights, some of us lads, who lived at Hingham, would meet outside the Unicorn pub, which was visited by many Americans, from whom we would always be given gum and candy. One night, I got into an argument with another lad called Charlie, when Mark Flaxman, the landlord, came out of the pub and said, 'Get on the Fairland and fight each other and I will give the winner two bob.' After I had hit the other lad with a straight left, he had had enough, so Mr Flaxman gave me two shillings and said that, when I was older, he would take me to a boxing club in Norwich. At that time, there would be a man with a cake van outside the pub selling biscuits and cakes, so I gave Charlie one of the shillings and we each had a bottle of ginger beer and a jam Swiss roll.

Les King, *King of Sport*, 1992

A water frolic

Barton Regatta on August Bank Holiday is possibly the most direct descendant, among all the Broadland regattas, of the water frolics depicted by the painters of the Norwich School. Nowhere else is there such yacht racing, with seventy or eighty sailing boast of all sorts and sizes, from punts and dinghies to topsail boats all entered in one race, and thirty or forty of them at a time sweeping down to the starting line in a tumult of foam and flapping canvas, avoiding collision by what looks like a succession of miracles. It is not a regatta to be recommended to an inexperienced helmsman, and even the expert is inclined to be a little deprecating about it, as an affair in which fortune as well as skill is necessary at the start, and he who gets away clear of the melee has the race already half won.

But all of them, the novices and the experts, come to Barton, and along with them comes the biggest assembly of cruising craft to be seen anywhere at one time on the Broads, to moor in the shallows while their crews watch the fun. For the object of Barton Regatta, over and above the racing, seems to be to enable as many people as possible to enjoy themselves on the water, and it is for that reason that it so truly deserves the title of a frolic.

The spectators as well as the competitors must be aquatic, for there is no land from which you can see Barton Broad. At other times than on August Bank Holiday it is the most secluded of the larger Broads, for the winding channel of the little River Ant is the only approach from the main rivers. From the landward, the best way is by an equally narrow and winding road to Barton Staithe, where bundles of reeds are piled ready for the thatchers, and where a cottage with an off-licence supplies refreshment for travellers. The beer is handed out of a barred window, and the customers satisfy the law by drinking it out of the neck of the bottle while sitting on a bench which is on the staithe but off the premises. This, oddly enough, is accepted as one of the curiosities of Barton – not of the licensing laws.

Jonathan Mardle, *Eastern Daily Press*, 8 August 1951

Amateur's expenses

It has always been a vexed question a to how far an amateur should be paid expenses when playing for his country or his county. It is now generally agreed that he should be paid all reasonable expenses. In the old days when the Norfolk cricket team played an out match we were allowed enough to cover rail fares and hotel expenses. This meant, as a rule, a grant of from two to three pounds per match. When that best and most generous of men, the late Mr. E. G. Buxton, was honorary treasurer, he was so honorary that it must have cost him a great deal of money. He was the great 'maker up of deficits'. I doubt if his like will ever be seen in Norfolk again, and the gap he left can never quite be filled.

On one occasion, a few days after a match at Cambridge, one of the most enterprising of our young players – whom I will call Sparrow – called in at the bank. 'Morning, Sparrow,' said E. G. 'What can I do for your?' Sparrow cleared his throat. 'It's – er – about my expenses to Cambridge, Mr Buxton,' he said. 'Oh, yes, of course, Sparrow. Let me see. How much do you want?' Sparrow gently mentioned the sum of *seven* pounds or so. 'Heavens! Sparrow, you can't have spent all that,' said E. G. 'Oh, but, Mr Buxton,' said Sparrow naïvely, '*you should just have seen the cards I held in the train!*' E. G. was so amused that, I am told, he paid up in full. He would.

B. Knyvet Wilson, *More Norfolk Tales and Memories*, 1931

Hold the back page!

All soccer scribes have horror stories of their own. Ted Bell once told me of an occasion when Norwich City were playing a non-League side in a Cup game, and he arrived at the ground to be presented with a brick and a long length of cord. Apparently the system was that the reporter wrote his copy, wrapped it round the brick, then lowered it out of the back of the grandstand where it was retrieved by a waiting boy who unwrapped the copy paper and ran to the nearest telephone. I recall two hair-raising incidents, one related to an away match played during a period of industrial trouble involving telephone operators. Some phone exchanges were working, and others were not, and the system had gone haywire. There was no operator to talk to, and for some reason the only direct dial connection I could make was not with the EDP office in Norwich but with an unknown lady in Rickmansworth. Whatever I dialled it was always the lady in Rickmansworth who answered. By the eighth or ninth connection, and against a background of my heightening tension and mumbled apologies, she finally professed a passing interest in the way the match was progressing. Not until early in the second half did I manage to establish a link with a frantic Pink Un staff in Redwell Street who were faced with empty pages, no match report, and time running out.

Another incident which did my blood pressure no good at all was an arrival in a Press box to find that although a booking had been made no phone was available. Nor was there the prospect of one. In the end I had to elicit the assistance of a 15-year-old lad sitting in the grandstand and persuade him, by the simple expedient of offering money, that he would be better employed as my 'runner'. I believe he made five trips out of the ground, clutching pages of my hasty handwritten scrawl, to a nearby telephone box to phone the copy through to Norwich. There was another moment of panic at a mid-week Combination match at Carrow Road, when there were a few fans on the terraces, only one or two in the grandstand and no-one else at all in the Press box. The goals started to flow with such regularity I dared not blink in case I missed one. When the final whistle went I calculated the result as 6–6, but having no one to check it with or talk to about it finally decided to find the referee. 'Was it 6–6?' I asked. 'I think so,' said the ref, adding, 'The players thought so, too, but I was going to have a word with the Press man.' I told him I was the Press man. In the end we compared notebooks, and agreed score and scorers.

Bruce Robinson, Passing Seasons, 1997

Hobbs at his best

After the Great War, Lionel Robinson and Archie MacLaren resumed the staging of top class country-house cricket matches on the beautiful ground at Old Buckenham Hall.

In 1921 they pulled off their biggest coup of all. Back in May 1919, Robinson's XII, captained then by J. R. Mason of Kent and including J. W. H. T. Douglas of Essex and the immortal Frank Woolley, had played a creditable draw with an Australian Imperial Forces' touring side packed with Test stars. However, it was the game in May 1921 that really caught the public's imagination when Robinson's XI met Warwick Armstrong's all-conquering Australians in the second match of their tour. Robinson's team, which MacLaren had assembled, boasted many of the day's top players, among them Chapman, Douglas, Fender, Hendren and the legendary Jack Hobbs.

On the first day of the historic match persistent rain allowed the bowling of only three overs, during which the Australians proceeded to 18 without loss.

By the following day the weather had improved and people flocked to Old Buckenham for 'one of the most wonderful days in the history of Norfolk cricket'. They arrived by pony and trap, horse and cart, motor cars, by bicycles and on foot. The roofs of some vehicles became temporary grandstands and the crowd was estimated at between 7,000 and 10,000 – the largest ever to watch a cricket game in Norfolk.

Despite Armstrong scoring 51 not out with some powerful drives and pulls, the mighty Australians were dismissed for a paltry 136, thanks largely to some fine seam bowling by John

Douglas, who bowled unchanged, and Clement Gibson of Sussex.

Then Hobbs took the stage and, for the next hour and a half, he enthralled the crowd with the ease and elegance of his batting. Withstanding the fast hostile deliveries of Gregory and McDonald, he reached 85 before the recurrence of leg muscle trouble forced him to retire. Like Jupp, the Sussex amateur who damaged a thumb, he took no further part in the match.

Despite these setbacks, MacLaren was able to declare at 256 for 7 on the third day, but the weather again intervened and the game fizzled out to a draw. In their curtailed second innings the Australians had their backs to the wall and the accurate Gibson recorded the remarkable figures of 9–8–1–1.

Although the weather was disappointing, the local press commented: 'To Norfolk the fixture has been a great and memorable event and the incidents of the match will be the gossip of the countryside and cricket pavilions for many years to come.' And so it proved to be.

Years later, in July 1952, Jack Hobbs visited Lakenham to renew acquaintance with Bill Fairservice, an old Kent player who at the time was scoring for Kent II. In the score-box keeping the records for Norfolk was Ken Hart, a prominent figure in Norfolk cricket circles for several decades. In 1921 Hart was headmaster of Old Buckenham School and during the famous match he had accommodated Hobbs and Hendren. To Hart's delight, Hobbs recalled the game, saying that the 85 he made against Gregory and McDonald on that occasion was one of the finest innings of his career. He added, 'They made me fight for every run.'

Philip Yaxley, *Looking Back at Norfolk Cricket*, 1997

Canaries on song

For once City found themselves on the receiving end; but so brilliant was Kennon's work that Luton were denied more than one goal, and Brennan celebrated his thirty-fourth birthday with an equalizer that took the semi-final into a replay at St Andrews, Birmingham.

That, alas, was the end of the road. There had been 63,500 at White Hart Lane. Nearly 50,000 went to Birmingham for the replay. They saw the Canaries dominate three parts of the game; but this time the Luton defence, supremely marshalled by Sid Owen, gave away nothing, and in the fifty-sixth minute Billy Bingham, the irrepressible Irishman, ended City's hopes of becoming the first side from the Third Division to appear at Wembley.

For half an hour after the match there were no dressing-room visitors. But if there was one asset the 1958/59 Canaries possessed in abundance it was character. On the way home in the 'Top Brass Special' – the railway phenomenon that blossomed during the Cup run – the City players moved from compartment to compartment chanting 'You sang for us, we'll sing for you!' And for disappointed supporters there was the bonus of chorus after chorus of 'On the Ball, City!' – sung by the Canaries themselves.

Ted Bell, *On the Ball, City*, 1972

On the ball, City!

In the days to call, which we have left behind,
Our boyhood's glorious game,
And our youthful vigour has declined
With its mirth and its lonesome end;
You will think of the time, the happy time
Its memories fond recall
When in the bloom of our youthful prime
We've kept upon the ball.

Kick off, throw it in, have a little scrimmage,
Keep it low, a splendid rush, bravo, win or die;
On the ball, City, never mind the danger,
Steady on, now's your chance,
Hurrah! We've scored a goal.

Let all tonight then drink with me
To the football game we love,
And wish it may successful be
As other games of old,
And in one grand united toast
Join player, game and song
And fondly pledge your pride and toast
Success to the City club.

Kick off, throw it in, have a little scrimmage,
Keep it low, a splendid rush, bravo, win or die;
On the ball, City, never mind the danger,
Steady on, now's your chance,
Hurrah! We've scored a goal.

The Norwich City Football Club 'anthem', penned by Albert Smith
and sung by supporters since the early years of the 20th century.

Record efforts

Some famous pedestrians have lived round Norwich. Brighten, 'the Milkboy,' Painter, and Joe Brown and others upheld the honour of the county in the days of the mighty 'Deerfoot.' Their exploits were crowned some twenty-five years since by the wonderful feats of members of the Fellowes and Upcher families. Old Mr. Upcher, of Kirby Rectory, could leap a big five-barred gate when he was seventy years of age. His sons, along with the Fellowes, represented their Universities and held championships. The most famous of all was the lamented Knyvet Upcher, who instituted the present style of hurdle-jumping. His great feats at Oxford and London were nothing to those he performed when he had retired from big meetings. He grew stronger, and increased all his records, though of course one cannot quote them as being authentic. I saw him at a country meeting jump 22 feet 10 inches on a soft grass track; this he supplemented by winning two hurdle races, in which he beat the best London men by a whole flight and more. He then threw the cricket ball 110 yards. I saw him in practice beat all present long-jump records by nearly a foot. Once he attempted a 30 foot marsh drain, and though he came flop in the water, yet his chest was against the bank. His stride when he took ordinary hurdles was frequently as much as 18 feet. Worthy successors to these giants of athletics have since held champion honours for the old county, such as C. G. Wood.

William Andrews (ed.), *Bygone Norfolk*, 1898

World Beater

Just picture those far-off days of pugilism when boxers fought for nothing like the fabulous sums some of the champions receive today. And in those days the fights were generally on the greensward in a 20-foot ring, and without the gloves.

Jem Mace was a Norfolk man, and the most remarkable champion of them all. He only stood five feet nine inches, and in his prime weighed no more than 10 stone 10 pounds.

Furthermore, he reigned as World Champion (with or without gloves) for many years, as his career touched the period of the Prize Ring with its bare-knuckle fights till it gave way to glove fighting as it is now known.

He was born at Beeston, near Swaffham, in Norfolk, in April, 1831, his father being the village blacksmith. For many years he lived in Norwich, and at one time was mine host of the 'Swan' tavern, which formerly stood in Swan Lane, Norwich. He died at the advanced age of 80 in Liverpool, and even in his later years was a remarkably well-preserved man of the dark handsome type, with a Romany appearance.

Although possessing no gypsy blood, he frequently, as a young man, toured the country with travelling fairs, where his skill at boxing quickly asserted itself. He was also no mean musician upon the fiddle – another of his accomplishments.

One of his most famous battles was with Sam Hurst, the 'Stalybridge Infant', who stood six feet two-and-a-half ins. and weighed no less than 17 stone. Hurst's admirers stated that the giant would 'squeeze the wee chap like a cooked turnip.'

Mace, however, was the victor in the eighth round after inflicting severe punishment upon Hurst.

In his prime, Mace combined both speed and terrific hitting power, and doubtless was one of the most skilful boxers who ever lived.

R. W. Stone, *The Norfolk Magazine*, 1951

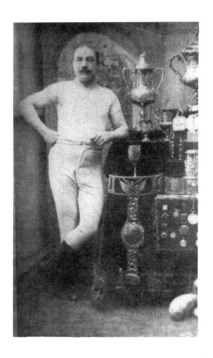

Jem Mace – Norfolk's World Champion

County crushed

We find a team calling itself 'Norfolk' taking the field for the first time in 1797, when a match between XXXIII of the county and XI of England took place on Swaffham Racecourse in the presence of an immense number of spectators from all parts of the Kingdom. The result of this match was rather disastrous for the county team, for they were beaten by an innings and 14 runs. In the two Norfolk innings of 50 and 80, there was but one solitary double-figure score (14 by Mitchell) and as many as 35 noughts! England, in their one innings, made 144, Tom Walker being top scorer with 55. One account reports the match to have taken three days, and another 'the greater part of a week'. No matter which of the two is correct, the scoring must have been somewhat slow. The result of the game seems to have put Norfolk cricketers in a rather chastened frame of mind, for a fair number of years elapsed before a team claiming to represent the county took the field again.

David Armstrong, *A Short History of Norfolk County Cricket*, 1990

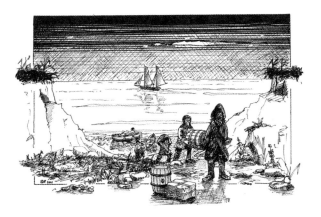

POACHERS AND SMUGGLERS

There's a tendency to treat poachers and smugglers with indulgent fondness, to cast furtive nocturnal characters as lovable rogues cocking a snook at the landed gentry and tax gatherers. In any case, genuine hardship rather than overblown greed was the main spur for such exploits in the darkness and undergrowth ...

This collection, featuring two classics of Norfolk literature from the 1930s, looks at life on both sides of the fence, turning from old family pastimes to augment meagre domestic rations to organised crime, vicious confrontations and death sentences.

Lilias Rider Haggard fashioned I Walked By Night *from the scribbled notes of the self-styled King of the Norfolk Poachers, Frederick Rolfe. Then she edited and shaped another outstanding work,* The Rabbit Skin Cap *from George Baldry's raw material. Impressive books still ensnaring readers with their simple directness and hardly littered with romantic traps.*

Her father, Henry Rider Haggard, the author of King Solomon's Mines, *and other memorable adventures, became a gentleman farmer on the Norfolk–Suffolk border ready to square up to grim realities of the countryside at the end of the Victorian era. As befitted a leading magistrate, he warned fervently against false sentiment being wasted on poachers, 'a band of thieving rascals'.*

A clever outlaw

As he walked along to work
And saw his landlord's game
Devour his master's crops,
He thought it was a shame.
But if the Keeper found on him
A rabbit or a wire;
He got it hot, when brought before
The Parson and the Squire.

Old Poaching Song

There was many a man asked me in those days what he had to learn to be a Professnial Poacher, and they mostly got the same answer. By experience he have to lern and he may lern a lot, but he want a lot of experence before he can become a fairly sucessful man. In them days I was not giving away anything, but now they are passed for me it dont matter, and I will try and tell most of what I lernt.

The first thing is to keep a still tunge in your head, as some young beginers get excited and begin to brag. Well nothing anoy a keeper more than to hear of some one bragin in a Public house of what he have done, and the keeper is shure to try and catch him, as he thinking his Master may hear of it and want to know why he is not looking after his business. Besides it let evryone know his trade and put People wise to him.

Its a true word that the days of the Professnial Poacher is gone. True there are a few pot hunters still about, but the young man of to day think more of his foot Ball and other kinds of sport, and I am not shure that they are not a lot better off.

Befor I have finished I think dear Reader you will agree that the Poacher is as clever as most other men. True he is an outlaw against the Laws of the land, but that do not disturb him much, but rather give him more encuragment than not.

If the Poacher work alone it is a hard Job for the Keeper to run him to earth, that is if the poacher use a little comon sence.

He will have a lot to lern as I have said befor. He must study wether, and all the signs of wood craft, the call of birds, and the flight of Wood Pigons in the wood at night, and distinguish the diffrent sounds, and there are a lot of diffrent sounds in the woods at night, and other rough places.

Wen he enters a wood he must get the wind in his face, and take pertucler notice wich point it blows from, or he is sone lost and must travel his ground over again, to no Purpose. The wind and the stars are his guide. If I was to sit down in the middle of a large wood and I could see the stars, I could easly find my way. Foggy wether is the worst the Poacher have to face, it may be clear wen he enter the wood, but the fogg lead him astray, and he may have a hard Job to find his way out. If he once loses himself he is lost, as evrything look alike to him.

A Poacher is worth all he get. A great many People would be surprised if they only knew what the poacher is asked to get for some People aspeshilly wen the game is out of season. A good many Farmers shut there eyes to the Poacher, they know he will shut the gates after him, beside them gettin a brace of Birds now and again. So long as the Poacher let his fowles alone he do not bother much about him. Also a good Poacher never disturb a flock of sheep if he can help it, as he know there is nothing for him were the sheep are folded. Some Shepperds are fool enough to try and give the Poacher away – silly on there part, as the Poacher can do him a lot of harm, and he is none the wiser till the harm is done.

Lilias Rider Haggard (ed.), *I Walked By Night*, 1935

A gruesome find

Of all the stories that persisted around the County's coastline, perhaps the strangest was one which was rife amongst the community of Happisburgh. During the early 19th century, the form of a man dressed in blue seafaring garb was reported to have been seen at dusk near Cart Gap. The spectre was particularly terrifying, for it was legless and its nearly severed head dangled horribly down its back. As weeks passed the story was almost forgotten until several homegoing farmworkers saw the apparition. They were so troubled by its hideous appearance that a number of them decided to lay in wait for it the following evening. As darkness fell the ghost again materialised from the direction of Cart Gap and made its way to a well on Happisburgh's pump hill. Here it thrust a large bundle it had been carrying down the shaft and then slowly followed into the murky depths.

A few days later the men brought the subject up at a parish meeting and, although ridiculed by fellow parishioners, they were promised help for searching the well. The next day a man was lowered into it, but after a lengthy search in the gloomy bottom, he shouted that he could find nothing and wished to be brought up. During the ascent he noticed a fragment of blue cloth hanging on the well side and, although still sceptical, agreed to make another search. Shortly afterwards the conversation of several onlookers was suddenly interrupted by a cry from the well which immediately made the men haul their comrade to the surface. He emerged, with a large but rotten bag, which revealed when untied a pair of legs that had been hacked off at the thighs. Villagers now watched a second man lowered down the shaft – for the original volunteer was too shocked to continue the search – and saw him bring up minutes later a partly decomposed body dressed in blue and with its head almost cut off.

After extensive local inquiries, it was discovered that these were almost certainly the remains of a smuggler who had been killed by his companions in a desolate bullock lodge near Cart Gap, and after being hacked apart was disposed of in the well.

R. E. Pestell, *Norfolk Fair*, July / August 1967

March 29, 1777 …Andrews the Smuggler brought me this night about 11 o'clock a bagg of Hyson Tea 6 Pd weight. He frightened us a little by whistling under the Parlour Window just as we were going to bed. I gave him some Geneva and paid him for the tea at 10/6 per Pd.

James Woodforde, *A Country Parson's Diary 1758–1802*

Snare for hare

Early one morning, I took one of the copper snares from the shed and hurried away to a thicket a mile or so from home. I was getting to know the ways of the hare by now. I chose a well-used run where fresh droppings showed it had been used earlier. I stopped up the hare's other runs so he would be sure to come along mine. I rubbed my hands along them and spat on them, then he wouldn't pass by my scent. Now he would be sure to come along the run I had chosen.

I set the snare as I had seen Pa do, just ahead of a pair of paw-marks on the run so his head would go through. I set it not too high or it would catch his front paws, nor too low or it would take his hind paws. I scattered a handful of leaves and leaf mould to cover sign of my meddling. Then I ran off and lay down in a nearby ditch to wait. I dozed in the ditch but I didn't have to wait more than an hour. I heard a quick squeal and knew the wire had hanged him.

Before Pa went out on his evening walk, I showed him my catch. The intimacy which I thought had grown between us was instantly gone.

'You will never do that again!' he said in a low and frightening tone.

In my pride at having trapped the hare with so little trouble, I had not bothered to notice that the animal, though hanged, was still breathing, its faint heart still beating. Through all the day hours since I first trapped it and hid it in the shed to show to Pa, it had been lying there, half alive.

Pa broke its neck. Then he took off his belt, pulled down my trousers, right there in the garden behind the cottage, and strapped my harder than he had strapped me for the truanting.

Rachel Anderson, *The Poacher's Son*, 1982

December 12th 1785 … Poor Tom Twaites of Honingham who was beat by the Poachers at Mr Townshends the other day is lately dead of the Wounds he then rec'd from them. His Skull was fractured in 2 places.

James Woodforde, *A Country Parson's Diary 1758–1802*

The Runner

'The Excise men, the Excise men,'
The lookout shouted clear.
'They're on the beam, I see the gleam
Of their lights. They're pulling near.'

'Avast and make the cargo fast
And stow that wicked sword;
For they must see us peacefully
Before they come aboard.'

The cutter with its curling bow
Drew near the runner's ship;
The waves ran high and made
The sky and bowsprit meet and dip.

But panic seized the smuggling men –
'Escape,' the brigand said.
He drew a gun, took careful aim
And shot the captain dead.

And off across the curling sea
The runners with their cargo fled;
Towards the Norfolk Coast they steered,
A price on each man's head.

'P. C.', *Norfolk Fair*, July / August 1967

Corruption ahoy!

Bribery and corruption in H. M. Customs were rife in Elizabethan times. Francis Shaxton of Lynn was one of England's greatest smugglers, abetted by local customs officials remote from central control, and he escaped punishment. John Wallis, leading merchant of Jacobean Lynn, seems to have avoided paying customs duties and export licences, apparently with the blessing of the Privy Council. In an effort to impose tighter controls on them, from 1565 provincial customs officials were obliged to keep port books.

Smuggling was inevitably encouraged by parliament's raising of duties on merchandise passing through England's ports. In 1711 duties were added on hides, coffee, tea, drugs, gilt, silver, wine and cocoa, and Lynn's customs officers were urged to be more vigilant. At this time they often seized brandy, wine, rum, paper, cloth and West Indian silks and spices. In 1716 the Board of Commissioners in London warned 'of ships hovering on the coast waiting for the opportunity to run their cargoes of brandy' and other goods and 'to carry off wool', implying local official were conniving in it.

Battles between smugglers and customs officials were frequent. The seizure of brandy in a Lynn house in 1718 led to a riot, the leaders of which were whipped round the town. In 1815 the revenue cutter attached to the Custom House captured a vessel off Hunstanton carrying 840 tons of geneva, and escorted it to the Purfleet. The smugglers were taken to the town gaol, from where they escaped through an open window into the night. In 1838 customs officers were more successful in discovering the smuggling of tobacco by carriers from Fakenham and Wisbech, who met at Lynn's *Maid's Head*. As free trade was gradually introduced by parliament from the 1830s and duties on imports and exports were reduced, smuggling became less profitable, but customs officials remained wary of licensing Lynn fishing boats if their owners were suspected of smuggling 'runs'.

Paul Richards, *King's Lynn*, 1990

Sentenced to death

The ultimate punishment of death was occasionally resorted to, though less frequently as time goes on, in cases in which poaching gangs were particularly violent..

Typical was the trial in 1824 of the poaching gang at Sprowston in which Miles Wiseman, Robert Whitaker, Henry Culley and Edmund Fisher were sentenced to death, for having shot at William Everett and March Buttifant with intent to murder them or do some grievous bodily harm. For when it came to the sentences being carried out, only Miles Wiseman was executed, to strike fear into the hearts of the rest, but the punishments of the others were unfortunately not recorded. Even then, Wiseman's fate was worsened, for 'the body of Miles Wiseman, who was executed at Thetford on April 10th for shooting at the gamekeeper at Rackheath, was stolen from Hardingham Church yard, a few nights after its internment, by some 'Resurrection men' who had been lurking about the chief part of the previous day.' Bodies were used for medical research, possibly at Cambridge University.

Michael J. Carter, *Peasants and Poachers*, 1980

'Worst characters'

It is extraordinary what an amount of false sentiment is wasted in certain quarters upon poachers, who, for the most part, are very cowardly villains, recruited from among the worst characters in the neighbourhood. When some friends and I hired the shooting at Bradenham, one of our keepers, a very fine young fellow named Holman, interrupted a gang of poachers engaged in killing pheasants at night. He was unarmed, and they were armed, and the end of it was that one of them escaped by throwing himself behind the trunk of a small tree. The man was identified, and tried at the Assizes, but as it was only 'a night poaching case,' a sentence of six months was thought to be sufficient punishment for this vigorous attempt at murder.

Not a year goes by without keepers, who are merely doing the duty for which they are paid, being murdered or beaten to a pulp by these bands of thieving rascals, who are out, not for sport, but for gain.

Henry Rider Haggard, *A Farmer's Year*, 1899

Secret tunnels

Kelling beach was a favourite landing place with its easy access to the hinterland. It was here, on February 28th, 1837 that Lieutenant George Howes and his men from Weybourne intercepted a large group of armed smugglers. In the ensuing 'most desperate affray' shotgun fire was exchanged and at least two of the smugglers were wounded – one seriously enough to have a leg subsequently amputated. The Coastguard men recovered five horses and six carts carrying 540 gallons of brandy and 3-4,000 pounds of manufactured tobacco. As with most coastal villages there are tales of secret tunnels and Weybourne is no exception. One is said to run under the church to the beach and it could be that if this is true then it could have connected with the second, that running from the old marl pit up the hill to the beach. Again, as at Salthouse and Cley, the millers may have helped things along by setting their sails in the form of a cross to warn the smugglers of impending danger, setting them going again when the way was clear.

Local legend has it that when a cargo was expected all those involved would go down to the beach and cover themselves with stones, with just their heads showing. In this way not only were they hard to see but if any uninvited stranger came along the sudden sight of bodies literally rising out of the beach was generally enough to scare them off!

Peter Brooks, *Weybourne*, 1984

'Honest' Hotching

Brancaster Staithe had a smuggler who became famous when he was finally caught, and ended his days – after some time spent at Her Majesty's pleasure – as an 'honest man' selling fish in the surrounding villages. He was William Hotching, who in the 1850s and 1860s kept a beer house named the *Hat and Feathers* in the easterly portion of what is now *The Hoe*, backing onto the marshes. At the height of his prosperity Hotching owned a lugger and a part share in a 50-foot cutter,

The Harlequin. These would meet Dutch boats out at sea and bring in cargoes, or 'crops' as he called them, of tobacco strip. He built a cellar behind the beer house and also had a large hiding place behind a chimney. At other times, local stories have it, his 'crop' was hidden in either marl or chalk pits or in a dip off the Whitehills road to Burnham Market which later became known as Thieves' Hole. When tides dictated a daylight operation, Hotching was said to have organised various events such as a bowling competition at the *White Horse* public house, so that all of the fishermen and their families would be occupied. He is reputed to have had a still in an outhouse of the property known as *The Palus.*

As his smuggling prospered, William Hotching took on several partners all of whom had good legitimate businesses in the neighbourhood. He himself would undertake delivery of the tobacco to clients, and kept a trap with a fast-trotting mare for the purpose. According to his story told to a reporter of the *Wide World* magazine, he covered 'the crop' in the trap with a layer of fish or shellfish, and was often stopped on his way to deliver his contraband by housewives wanting his fish. The tale is told in the village that one day he and his trap were chased by 'the preventives' as he called the excisemen, along the road from Docking to Bircham Newton that leads to Great Bircham. At the point in the road where there is a deep dip he was able to give the heavier and more unwieldy law enforcement vehicle the slip as his fleetfoot mare took him quickly out of their reach. Another tale is that Hotching once paid a shepherd £5 – probably about a year's wages at the time – to take his flock of sheep up and down a telltale track on the marshes north of the *Hat and Feathers* so as to obliterate the signs that a large haul of tobacco had been brought from what is now known as Smuggler's Gap, along Stone Creek and so to the marshside cart road and his beer house.

In 1865 or 1866 Hotching and his partners, always searching for new outlets for their tobacco – and changing delivery dates and areas was part of their evasion tactics – were caught in a trap in King's Lynn. As he was delivering a load of tobacco to a new client, the 'preventives' dropped on him as he passed under the south gate arch of the town. He and his fellow smugglers were convicted and fined £840 each or six months in prison – a surprisingly lenient end to what must have been a long career as a smuggler. They chose to go to prison. When he was freed Hotching found that his fortune had been dissipated in some way not explained in the *Wide World* article. Although there were pressures on him to take up smuggling again he elected to 'go straight', and was a shellfish merchant for the rest of his working life. He used often to call at the coffee house known as *The Plough* at Burnham Deepdale. The Riches family who ran it recounted how William Hotching used to tell them stories of his smuggling days and say, 'I've had milkpails of money through my hands'. His son, Sheldrake, born when his father was 60, was known as Shelley, and regaled his fellow villagers of Staithe with many tales of his father. Shelley spent his working life as a policeman.

Maurice de Soissons, *Brancaster Staithe,* 1993

December 29th, 1786 … Had another Tub of Gin and another of the best Coniac Brandy brought me this Evening ab' 9. We heard a thump at the Front Door about that time, but did not know what it was, till I went out and found the 2 Tubs – but nobody there.

James Woodforde, *A Country Parson's Diary 1758–1802*

Artful as foxes

It was a grand night with a light breeze a-blowing towards the wood. There weren't nothing wrong with the Snobs' ears and they hears the Cop talking and me a-clattering down the road, and there they was with the pockets of their frock coats bulging with pheasants. They decided to take a short cut across the fields, one saying:

'Du yew take my bards while I goes in front, and keep yew close to the fence and a nice distance behind. If I comes across any one I'll shew fight and yew'll know what's a' clock.'

Off they goes, as artful as foxes and soon manages to git

back to their shanty with a good haul and never a sign of Cop nor keepers. They see me and one of them held up his hand and scowled at me to keep quiet while they unloaded their pockets, me a-looking on. They moved an old chest standing in a corner, took up some bricks from the floor, scrabbed away the soil lifting a lid set in a wood frame that covered a hole big enough from one of the Snobs to hide in. In went the haul of pheasants and some more odd things that I did not understand at the time, but found out later.

They were old tins that had been used to keep thin sticks of rock in, which were sold at four a penny when I was a boy, about twelve inches long and two inches across the top. They made some small holes all round about an inch from the bottom, fastened the tin to a two foot stick, then socketed three or four more. The lot could then be carried with the ends resting in the coat pocket and when the coat was buttoned up no outsider would be the wiser.

When the Snobs had a mind to have a ramble at night during the shooting season this peculiar contrivance went with them, as they knew very well if they carried a gun and fired that off they would not get very far. Just before they started they used to put some rags in the bottom of the tin and sprinkle some sulphur on top.

Generally Calico Jack took the tin and stowed it away with some sulphur matches, the sort that had to be held at arm's length or you'd be suffocated, but they'd give a light in a second. My grandmother used to think they was the most wonderful things after she had been striking her flints for hours to get a spark into her tinder box, and I have often heard her say the man who invented the first match – something that would light by just rubbing it – had a good head on him, and, if she knew him, she'd give him a good hug and a kiss. She would have, too, being one of them spit-fire old ladies good enough for anything in her day.

Was now getting on with my education and beginning to see things as they were and not as they appeared. Knew how Calico Jack and his company got their haul so quickly.

When there was a lot of birds sitting on the low branches all they had to do was light up the sulphur under an old coat and when it got going hold it under the pheasant. The silly bird sitting with outstretched neck to see what was doing down below, was soon knocked out and down he come, his neck was wrung and he was bagged in a hurry, for it was not the custom of the Snobs to let the grass grow under their feet.

If their ways were looked at in the right light they were made what they had become, getting only a bread and cheese living – the cheese hard to see sometimes – and also there is a saying ,'Get old – get artful.'

They was out night after night giving Cops and keepers a time, and most occasions would get clear away with it.

Lilias Rider Haggard (ed.), *The Rabbit Skin Cap*, 1939

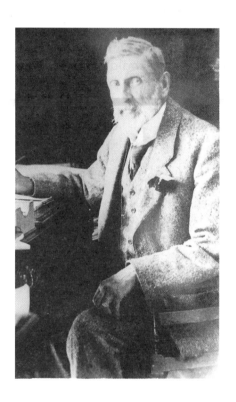

Henry Rider Haggard

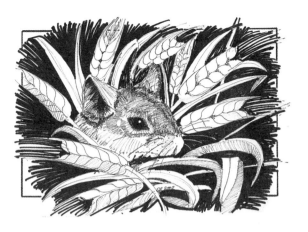

BIRDS, BEASTS AND FLOWERS

Norfolk has been singularly fortunate in bringing forward outstanding naturalists able to communicate their energy, enthusiasm and expertise in print. This section emphasises that richness of talent … while offering an apology for not having sufficient scope to feature it all. It is simply representative of a remarkable breed of men and women.

Master and disciple, learning and sharing by observation, lead the way. Arthur Patterson, writing for local papers under the typically self-effacing name of John Knowlittle, was a self-taught naturalist who became an authority on Breydon Water, the estuary at Yarmouth which inspired his 1929 classic, Wild Fowlers and Poachers. *It was typed at his dictation by a young follower called Ted Ellis, himself destined to be another leading Norfolk personality.*

The old man maintained that a true naturalist should always be ready to share his pleasure with others. If communication was Patterson's gospel, it was certainly the Ellis gift, not least as a popular radio and television broadcaster, as well as a prolific columnist in local and national publications.

Ted Eales followed his father as warden at Blakeney Point and also became a well-known countryman on local television. Bob Chestney was warden of Scolt Head, the island of terns. Both recounted their outdoor adventures to provide colourful and valuable records of changing fortunes on Norfolk nature reserves.

The Norfolk Sheep

'The Norfolk sheep are the worst in Britain', said Robert Bakewell. Billy Coke of Holkham heeded his words, and kept Southdowns, Leicesters and Lincolns – Whiggish sheep as a Tory lady called them, complaining that mutton had lost its flavour. But, about 50 years later somebody wrote 'The men of Norfolk and Suffolk know their business too well to make it safe to assume that these sheep are as bad as they. (Sheep bred from a Norfolk ram and Southdown ewe were afterwards called Suffolk.)

By the middle of the last century the original Norfolk sheep had become rare. Once they had reigned supreme, the horned, black-faced breed of the wilderness. Over much of the country the heath stretched as far as the eye could see, free and sweet-scented in the sunshine. Here and there were patches of cropped lawn, long grasses and flowers by the tinkling streams. A rough road led to a few fields about a village. People went their way contentedly in the summer, but the shades of winter scarcity were ever present. In a dark hovel, a sick man groaned. At the cross-roads a corpse hung from the gibbet.

The sheep were even older than the landscape. Of restless habit, they were sometimes 'ill-formed, unquiet beasts', but famous for hardiness, endurance of driving, and as nurses. Moreover, their wool was judged the third best in England, and the taste of the mutton was unsurpassed. The tallow they yielded was useful in candles. But, during the eighteenth century 'improvers' had changed much of the Norfolk scene, turning heath into arable fields, and pastures, planting trees, and building fine houses and buildings.

With the change of scene came a change of sheep. But some waxed hot in defence of the Norfolks. Nathaniel Kent, the agriculturist said they were 'as natural to the soil as the rabbits, being hardy in their nature, and of agile construction, so that they can move over a great space with little labour' He stressed the aid they had given to the new improvements, by fetching their sustenance from a considerable distance. 'Notwithstanding this there are some gentlemen, and some considerable farmers too, who begin to dislike and despise them, and prefer the Leicester and Lincoln breeds, but the

Norfolk farmer will never be able to substitute any other sheep that will answer penning so well.'

Yet the old Norfolk way of life was doomed, and with it the sheep. By 1847 'the restless Norfolk was rarely seen at any rate in the South of East Anglia.' The Suffolks had taken their place, and had proved to be equally hardy, thriving on dry soils. The magnificent horns of the Norfolks had been bred out, symbolic of much of the beauty and brutality of older times. Here and there a few flocks remained in the possession of farmers who harked back to the methods of their fathers, or were interested in keeping the historic breed in existence. Thus, it survived for another century, in increasingly few numbers. Nowadays, sad to say, Norfolks only survive at Whipsnade Zoo.

Jane Hales, *The East Wind*, 1969

Arriving by night

I shook myself from my thoughts because the wind was shrieking into my ears once more reminding me that I was getting very cold standing in such an exposed position. Turning, I walked back to the beginning of the reserve, resolving to come back at night for this reason. There are huge flocks of pink feet geese that come to this part of the Wash and to several of the very large fields around here for the winter months. You can hear them in the distance sometimes as they drop down onto the muddy earth that has been rich with sugar beet, and potatoes, and now winter wheat showing. They feed on these and seem to enjoy their diet immensely. But I wanted to see if it was possible to have a glimpse and hear the sound of a fresh migrating flock as they arrive by night.

So with the approaching tide and with the darkness closing in around me, I returned to this long shingle spit. The wind had died down considerably, once more giving me the chance to see the velvet night sky with stars again showing brightly. I settled myself in the shelter of a large clump of marram grass and prepared to wait. Warmly clad, I had a flask of hot drink with me. I had not so very long been sitting there when away in the very far distance I heard a faint, faint sound. This rapidly grew to calls I can only describe to you as exactly resembling a pack of baying hounds on the scent. It was, to be sure, a huge flock of pink feet coming in for the first time to drop down onto the water. There they would remain for the rest of the night.

These birds keep in touch with each other as they fly through the darkness. Their calls always seem to be anxious cries to make sure that they are not alone; that their companions are around them. It is a thrilling sound and one that has never ceased to affect me very greatly as the very essence of wild untamed life. This would be the first time that this particular flock had arrived here. Normally as soon as the day-light came they would be up and finding the fields, probably the same fields as they had used the previous winter for feeding. This is one of the fantastic features of migration travel. Birds will return to the same area and some even, as we know with swallows, to the same building as they have known the previous summer.

Hugh Brandon-Cox, *Mud on my Boots*, 1994

Spot the intruder

If a stoat, weasel or rat hunted the ternery in daylight, terns (especially common), skylarks and meadow pipits warned of the intruder. They hovered over it in considerable numbers, calling and following it as it hunted. I have even seen common terns hover over a long-tailed fieldmouse, especially immediately after rain at the end of a dry spell when it had been tempted out in daylight by the smell of moisture. These birds will hover over any strange new object, only dispersing after establishing that it is harmless, or if there is a lack of movement.

On one occasion, after several days of northerly winds and waves almost reaching the dunes, the terns were to be seen continually hovering in the same spot. I investigated several times in the space of an hour, but saw neither movement not anything alarming. I finally decided to stay forty yards away from the place of attraction, to watch and wait. Within seconds of my sitting down the terns returned and hovered over the same spot as before. I still could see no movement or danger; so, pin-pointing the exact spot, I went to investigate. Lying on the sand, sealed in a polythene bag, I found a koala. With its black plastic feet and life-like eyes this furry cuddly toy looked alive even to me – how much more so to a tern! No doubt it had been washed onto the beach – but from where? I gave it to Sally, to whom it became a great treasure. (It is still in the family today, being the proudest possession of her daughter!)

A hedgehog was a surprise cause of commotion in the ternery. At the time this was a rare species; so after being caught it was taken to the observation hut and placed in a fish box. When I returned home I put it my side-bag but during the walk back a considerable number of fleas decided to desert their host and crawl onto me. On reaching Dial House I placed the bag near the back door and hurried to change my shorts and pullover; after which, placing the hedgehog in a polythene bag in the boot of the car, I took it to the edge of the common, where I released it. Over the next three or four days I had to de-flea the cat and the two spaniels, as they were forever scratching! This was the only hedgehog recorded on Scolt, or at least in the sixty-one years that Chesneys were wardens. How did it get there?

Bob Chestney, *Island of Terns*, 1993

Frantic swifts

To me the most amazing thing was the spectacle of the swifts. It was late for them, near the end of August; they should now have been far away on their flight to Africa; yet here they were, delaying on that desolate east coast in wind and wet, more than a hundred of them. It was strange to see so many at one spot, and I could only suppose that they had congregated previous to migration at that unsuitable place, and were being kept back by the late breeders, who had not yet been wrought up to the point of abandoning their broods. They haunted a vast ruinous old barn-like building near the front, which was probably old a century before the town was built, and about fifteen to twenty pairs had their nests under the eaves. Over this building they hung all day in a crowd, rising high to come down again at a frantic speed, and at each descent a few birds could be seen to enter the holes, while others rushed out to join the throng, and then all rose and came down again and swept round and round in a furious chase, shrieking as if mad. At all hours they drew me to that spot, and standing there, marvelling at their staying power and the fury that possessed them, they appeared to me like tormented beings, and were like those doomed wretches in the halls of Eblis whose hearts were in a blaze of unquenchable fire, and who, every one with hands pressed to his breast, went spinning round in an everlasting agonised dance. They were tormented and crazed by the two most powerful instinct of birds pulling in opposite directions - the parental instinct and the passion of migration which called them to the south.

W. H. Hudson, *Afoot in England*, 1909

Dreaming

A tabula rasa
Settles on White Cast
Marshes where frost fingers
Grip a slate-grey dyke,

As Grandfather Heron
Defies an East Wind
In his grey woollen coat
By the still waters
Frozen in time. He waits,
With his dreams drifting
Over a sleeping realm.
He waits, and watches

The pale colours pinned
In a crystal sky
So far beyond the reach
Of his darting beak,

Old Heron reads the runes
In wrought iron trees,
And he hears the dry bone
Rattle of dead reeds,

Recalls all the omens,
He marks out the time
And waits. Silent. Alone.
Gathering magic

To dream out his patterns
Across this cold sky,
Awakening the green
Deep in the Heartwood.

pHIL nICHOLLS, *The Dreams of Grandfather Heron*, 1999

Forest newcomers

Red, roe and fallow deer are all to be found in the forests but
are very shy of human beings and careful stalking has be
undertaken if the naturalist hopes for the thrill of watching
these graceful animals at close quarters. Travellers along the
beautiful Breckland roads do occasionally have the good
fortune to see one of these animals crossing the road ahead of
them. The red deer are probably descendants of outliers from
the Norwich Stag Hunt, while the roe are almost certainly
descendants of a few pairs that were introduced to the Suffolk
area by a sporting gentleman about 1884. They were at first
kept in a specially constructed deer pen but later released, when
they increased considerably and were soon well established in
the Breckland forests. Fallow deer made their appearance
during the First World War when some escaped from the

Suffolk estate of Livermere and they also quickly settled in these woodlands.

A newcomer which was first reported in Breckland three years ago is a little deer called the Muntjac. Its arrival is rather mysterious, as no one can say at present from whence it came. Standing somewhat less than two feet high it is easily overlooked and anyone getting a good view of one of these most charming little animals could count themselves most fortunate.

Foxes are quite numerous, especially in the Stanford battle training area where for several years they bred unmolested. Red squirrels were plentiful but for how long remains to be seen, as the larger grey species which recently made its appearance in Suffolk has this winter been observed on the Norfolk side of the border and it is feared that it may in time exterminate the beautiful little red animal.

A third newcomer to Breckland in recent years is the coypu, a native of South America. This animal, which is bred in England in captivity for its pelts, escaped from one of the coypu 'farms' a few years ago and was soon breeding in such natural surroundings as the Norfolk Broads. After steadily extending its range it has now colonised some of the Breckland waters.

There are but very few reports of the badger being seen but the otter appears to have increased in recent years, probably because the otter hounds that were kennelled near Watton between the wars are now but a memory.

George Jessup, *East Anglian Magazine*, April 1957

Writing it down

Winds, tides, weather and migration ruled Arthur's direction, whether he went to beach, river walls or the Breydon marshes. He watched the birds, often with evil intent, but in striving to outwit and over-reach them he picked up, unconsciously, much about their habits and ways; and, in so doing, came across many a strange insect or fish. His earliest ambition was to write a book on Yarmouth birds.

Early one May morning, when out on Breydon, he fastened his punt to an old hulk on Breydon to take a look at waders using the mudflats as halfway house on their spring migration. He climbed aboard the old ship and lay in the sunshine. Presently a swallow, then another, flew out of the open hatch, and going in, he discovered a nest. There, in the middle of the vast estuary, the swallows brought off their young.

When Arthur saw a letter in 'The Standard' from a gentleman who expressed surprise at seeing a kingfisher in the very heart of London, he was prompted to reply. On September 19th, just before his 21st birthday, his first contribution to the Press appeared in that paper. He spoke of the number of kingfishers that could be seen on Yarmouth denes, and accounted the story of the swallows' nest he observed on Breydon. Seeing his name in print was a new experience and he so cherished his first contribution that he obtained a 'notebook' and pasted it therein. The letter was to be the forerunner of many hundreds of newspaper articles. In the same year Arthur began jotting down observations in his nature notebook after J. H. Gurney, F.L.S., F.Z.S., the naturalist, pointed out to him the importance of dating all incidents and records. Arthur Patteson was to write 44 diaries in the course of his lifetime and they are now in the custody of the Norfolk Record Office.

Beryl Tooley, *John Knowlittle, the Life of the Yarmouth Naturalist*, 1985

Churchyard charms

It is the middle of the afternoon and I am sitting in a favourite place ... on an old wooden seat deep among the grasses in Hethel churchyard – God's untrimmed acre.

In this hallowed place there is peace and tranquillity, solitude and silence. Few would know of this churchyard, for the lane that leads to this church goes nowhere else in particular.

At my feet are bush vetches, clustered with purple flowers being visited by bumble-bees – experts in opening the pea-shaped blossoms. I notice some of their pollen baskets are laden, ready for the return trip to the nest.

The wind blows through the churchyard and all the moon-daisies and the grasses lean aslant gracefully. What a paradise for wild things is this consecrated place of straightened and tipsy tombstones. I leave the old wooden seat and wander round the churchyard. Everywhere there is wilderness. Eye-level wilderness. How we need wilderness in our root-starved lives.

I pass a thrush's anvil at the base of the walls of the church, scattered with the remains of prettily banded snails. I pass arching sprays of dog roses with pink-tipped buds. I stop to look at ground elder flowers, the leaves at one time considered such a delicacy – boiled like spinach and eaten with butter.

Enamel-blue damselflies are resting among the grasses, brilliant and delicately gauzy. I stop to smell huge flat creamy heads of elder flowers – their heavy-sweet musky scent so attractive to the senses. I notice there are banded snails among the cow parsley – the thrush with the anvil knows where to find its food!

Lacy umbels of hogweed smell strongly of the cow-house. A wren pierces the silence of the churchyard with its penetrating trilling. How aromatic are the leaves of ground-ivy, deep among the grasses. Waxy-chaliced buttercups gild the grasses here and there. What a sanctuary the churchyard is for the life of the wild.

The field maple in the church hedgerow is reddened with leaf galls, and leaf coils dangle from the hazels, the quaint little homes of the larvae of leaf-rolling weevils. Thistles near the church door, which is a riot of roses, are soon to be crowned with purple, and amethyst pin-cushions of field scabious are waiting in bud.

An angel among the grasses is encrusted with orange lichens. I remove some of the mosses at its base to find a clue to its age. The statue is dated, the Good Friday of 1914.

My forty minutes away from the world is over. I open the gate to leave the churchyard. It wails with a melancholy iron squeak, as it always has done. I close the gate and drop the latch. God's in his heaven in his untrimmed acre …

Rosemary Tilbrook, *A Year in the Countryside*, 2000

The Little Gal's Rabbit

That died today,
That little white rabbit,
An she set here an cried.
That were her own,
Her pet, that rabbit;
She loved it. Then that died.

Poor little mawther,
She's on'y saven;
In't naathin' yew can say.
Tha's allus haard
T'larn, y'know ....
God give: God taake away.

John Kett, *Tha's a Rum'un Tew!*, 1975

Causing a flutter

September of course was a great month for migration and all
these bird watchers would stay at Cley and Blakeney. Many
bird watchers stayed at the George Hotel at Cley and I was in
close contact with some of them. If we had a rarity in the bushes
in the morning, when I looked out first thing, I would ring up
the George Hotel and tell them what we had got on Blakeney
so that they could come and have a look if they wanted to.
These were the first 'twitchers' if you like to call them such,
and they would come along the beach and look for the odd
bird.

On one occasion I got sadly wrong with the landlady of the
George Hotel. She was a great sport and she liked me to ring
up her guests and tell them of the birds that were about, but
on this occasion I put my foot right in it. I rang up at lunch-
time and said, 'Oh, Mrs. Burdett, there's a nice bluethroat just
come in the bushes and I don't know whether your guests have
seen one this year, but if they want to see one they can come
along and see it any time now because he will probably be

there for an hour or two.' Of course, unwittingly, she went into the dining-room when the soup was just being served and she said, 'Oh, Ted has just rung up, there's a bluethroat on the Point.' Without more ado the dining-room was evacuated immediately, everybody deserted the George and came down to Blakeney Point. My name wasn't worth mentioning in the George by the landlady or my wife, because they were both preparing lunch and I upset the apple-cart, or should I say the landlady did because she didn't realise what a bluethroat was. If she had done she would never have mentioned it until lunch was finished.

Ted Eales, *Countryman's Memoirs*, 1986

Hovering harriers

As we were coming home, past the long stretch of salt marsh, where the sinking sun flung wide shafts of light over the dark pools and lit the masses of marsh sorrel to a ruddy crimson, we saw a pair of harriers hovering over a distant reed bed. One dropped almost at once, but the other, the falcon by its size, soared and swooped and hung in the still air for about five minutes before she joined her mate in the reeds. These big hawks are a lovely sight in flight, and one that may grow more common with the passing months, for the marsh roads are labelled with notices 'No Access to Beach' and the rare birds which haunt this stretch of coast have once again the chance of privacy which alone saves them from extinction at the hands of the wandering gunner.

A little further on a flock of starlings suddenly surged over the rising ground behind, and poured down upon the marsh towards their roosting-place in the reed beds. They settled for a moment, a black cloud fallen from the sky upon the still brilliant grass, then swept up in perfect unison of movement. Thousands of apparently leaderless birds moved by a single mind, tilting and swerving at terrific speed, changing direction and formation with every second, until suddenly the whole compact wave swooped downwards, burst into a thousand entities, and settled amid the greys and golds of the bending reeds.

Then the silent marsh broke into a babel as a couple of thousand throats chinked and purred and bubbled and whistled, a confused medley of sound from which fell suddenly, like drops of water, the wilder notes of sea birds and waders. Notes with which the starling, master mimic that he is, mocks us from the chimney-pots some hot summer morning in the depths of the town.

Lilias Rider Haggard, *A Country Scrapbook*, 1950

Trumpet blasts

Surlingham, December 2nd, 1952. One morning during the past week we were awakened soon after five o'clock by the trumpet notes of whooper swans as the great birds flew just above our house in brilliant moonlight.

There is magic in the wild night music of pipers on the mudflats, peewits skirling on stony fields, curlews travelling high above the silver river, and grey geese loudly gossiping and squabbling on their journeys to and from the coast. There is mystery in many a strange cry, squeak or whistle heard in the fog of an autumn night when migrant birds are on the move in their thousands. There is pure glory in the whispering, trilling, fluting chorus that welcomes the day's awakening in spring. There is poignancy in the strange utterances of all fowls of the air at times when they are rejoicing in domestic bliss and coquetry. A signal of ancestral fear is aroused by the screeching and wailing of owls when night clouds ink the skies and the pollard oak assumes distorted human shapes. But in all my experience of bird music, never have I heard anything so deeply stirring as the bold and measured trumpet blasts of those moon-silvered swans when they swept so close to us as to disturb our slumbers all unwittingly the other morning.

Ted Ellis, *Countryside Reflections*, 1982

95

Pigs' Pleasure

April 15, 1778 ... Brewed a vessell of strong Beer today. My two large Piggs, by drinking some Beer grounds taking out of one of my Barrels today, got so amazingly drunk by it, that they were not able to stand and appeared like dead things almost, and so remained all night from dinner time today. I never saw Piggs so drunk in my life. I slit their ears for them without feeling.

April 16, 1778 ... My 2 Piggs are still unable to walk yet, but they are better than they were yesterday. They tumble about the yard and can by no means stand at all steady yet. In the afternoon my 2 Piggs were tolerably sober.

James Woodforde, *A Country Parson's Diary 1758–1802*

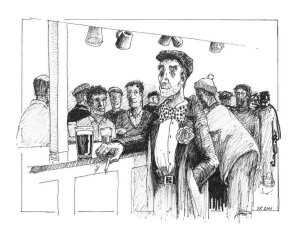

COLOURFUL CHARACTERS

Plenty of jostling in the wings for a place on stage with the cream of Norfolk's characters. Inevitably, a host of worthy – and not-so-worthy – candidates have to wait for another production while this select troupe present their telling routines.

I looked for touches of originality and eccentricity in their make-up, enough to make them stand out even in a colourful crowd. The Rector of Stiffkey, surrounded by fallen women, and 'Mad' Windham of Felbrigg Hall, crippled by debt and debauchery, soon pushed through to earn a measure of sympathy to go with automatic chastisement.

Poor Wolf-Charlie, one of Mary Mann's grimmest creations on her memorable rural canvas, stands alongside Jerry Eke, champion eater on the harvest supper scene. Tree worshipper, Edward Rigby, compares notes with 'Scientific' Fuller, self-styled King of Rockland Broad.

There's also room for the Sheringham nightsoil man and a farmer for whom witchcraft was no laughing matter over a century ago.

Prostitutes' Padre

Harold Davidson (1876 - 1937), who obtained the living of the remote Norfolk parish of Stiffkey in 1906, began early to show the interest in fallen girls which eventually led to his own downfall. Before the First World War he would make fortnightly visits to Paris in search of suitable girls to rescue. After the war and throughout the 1920s he continued his mission in London, travelling there before dawn on Monday mornings and not returning until late of Saturdays, spending night and day at his missionary work. He was proud, he later said, to be called the 'Prostitutes' Padre'.

Others thought less well of him; investigators were hired to follow him and one of them, after feeding a certain Rose Ellis eight glasses of port, extracted a scandalous story from her. Davidson wrote letters in his own defence, Rose Ellis withdrew her accusation, but not in time to prevent Davidson publishing his full story in the *Empire News*. By now the press were accusing him of immoral practices with over a thousand girls. His fame grew, his church congregation at Stiffkey swelled to 500, and in February 1932 one coach-load travelled from as far as Bournemouth to hear him preach.

Davidson was brought before the Consistory Court, sitting in the Great Hall of Church House, Westminster. Here his trial lasted over four months and was reported at length each day in the press. In June when the chancellor retired to consider his summing up, Davidson returned to Stiffkey and ejected a clergyman sent to minister in his absence. Later that month he was granted permission to give recitations to audiences of up to two thousand at Birmingham.

When the court found him guilty on all five charges he went to Blackpool and sat in a barrel for fourteen hours a day to raise money for his appeal. He was fined for obstruction. Returning once more to Stiffkey, he was kicked down the front steps by his churchwarden, Major Hammond. The Major was fined twenty shillings for assault.

On the day of his ceremonial defrocking at Norwich Cathedral, Davidson sent a telegram to say he would be late. Then when he arrived, he continuously interrupted the bishop during the proceedings. In the procession to the high altar he forced his way forward and supplanted the bishop.

Three years later in the summer of 1935 Davidson and his daughter Pamela returned to Blackpool to enter adjoining fasting cages. They were arrested and charged with attempted suicide, but the charge failed and Davidson was awarded £382 damages against Blackpool Corporation. At Skegness Amusement Park in the summer of 1937, when speaking to the public from inside a lion's cage, the lion, whose name was Freddie, attacked him and severely injured his head and neck. Freddie's keeper, sixteen-year-old Irene, rescued Davidson but he died two days later in Skegness Cottage Hospital.

Thomas Hinde, *The English Country Parson*, 1983

Clifftop drama

Yarker bought them all a round of beer and sat down next to Tebbutt. Clenchwarden sank back on his bench, unwilling to catch his ex-employee's eye and tried to drown himself in his shandy.

'I done well this afternoon,' Yarker told his employee, genially. 'Bought a whole load of furniture off of an old girl Dereham way who didn't know no better. Drove it round to a mate of mine in King's Lynn and sold it all for ten times as much. Well, eight or nine. Not bad for one afternoon, hey, bor?'

'Who was that then, Greg?' asked Burton.

'Woman name of Fox, whistles when she talks, looks at you out of one eye, keeps an old dog who smells like a bit of used toilet paper.'

The ferret man laughed heartily. 'That's my missus's aunt, Dot Fox. Funny thing happened to her some years back when she was married. She used to live over Happisburgh way, woke up one morning and found her back garden had fallen over the cliff. Apparently she'd been drinking so heavy the night before, she slept through one of the worst storms on the coast for twenty years. What was funny, was her husband Bert had gone out in his nightshirt to see to the chickens, what they kept in the garden shed, and he went over the cliff edge with the rest of 'em. Three in the morning, it was.'

Everyone present roared with laughter. The ferret man followed up his success with a postscript. 'They found Bert washed up on Mundesley beach a week later, they did, still wearing his nightshirt. Old Dot Fox kept that nightshirt for years as a souvenir. She's probably still got it, 'less you bought it off her, Greg.'

More laughter, and more drink called for.

Brian Aldiss, *Remembrance Day*, 1993

'Lijah's Hosses

'Cup, cup ...cup-whoa!' ... I haard the hosses tarn
An' stop, not far away from ar back door.
Then 'Lijah come up close agen the hedge;
I'd hear him holler, 'Wha's o'clock then, bor?'
An' I'd run in an' look at that ole clock;
There in the corner on a shelf that stood.
Then back I'd go, an' shout, 'Tha's jus' gone twelve',
An' 'Lijah, he'uld holler back, 'Tha's good!'
Then he'd git out the hosses'nosebags fust,
Afore he set right down agen them trees,
Took out 'is knife, a hunk o' crusty bread,
An' cut hisself a tidy lump o'cheese.
Not long he'd set there, 'fore he up agen,
Han's t'the plough, his back a little bent;
'Cup, cup there – wheesh!' I watched the furrer shine
Behind the team, as crorst the field they went,
Wi' flutt'rin' flocks o' seagulls allus nigh,
An' cryin' peewits tumblin'in the sky.

John Kett, *Tha's a Rum'un, Bor!*, 1973

Jerry tucks in

Somewhere in the neighbourhood of Aylsham lived a certain Jerry Eke, whose appetite was said to be superhuman, and whose prowess at harvest suppers was the boast and wonder and envy of the villagers round. It came to pass that at a farmers' market dinner the talk turned upon Mr. Eke's performances, when some one present protested that what had been narrated was impossible.

'Impossible!' said another. 'I'll bet you five pounds Jerry Eke will eat a calf at a sitting.' The wager was taken, and the preliminaries were arranged. The calf – let us hope only a baby calf – was killed; the bones were cut out, the flesh was chopped into minute particles, and apportioned into seventeen enormous pasties, whose outer crust was a thin film of batter made lovely and tempting to every sense, but carefully kept from any ingredients that could cloy the palate. Jerry was called in, he having agreed to the wager with evident delight, and was told he might fall to. He did so, and steadily gorged. He had made no difficulty of the first nine pasties, but when a tenth was brought in he seemed to flag. To the horror of his backers, he sighed and looked perplexed. It was but for a moment; he desired only to expostulate: 'I say, Mas'r, I ain't got nothing to say agin them poys, I loik 'em amazin'; but I'm a thinkin' et's abaywt time as I should begin upon that there calf!'

Augustus Jessopp, *Arcady: For Better For Worse*, 1887

Tree worshipper

Reference books will inform you about Edward Rigby's life as a doctor in the Norfolk and Norwich Hospital, but I have yet to come across one book which deals with the folk tales regarding his life at Framingham Earl. Local lore includes a lot of details regarding the things he did when living at the Old Hall. He not only ran a smallpox hospital there. He, being a man who believed that trees had life just like human beings, was in effect a tree worshipper. In furtherance of this cult, he turned people out of the cottages on his estate; pulled the houses down, then planted trees on the site. He was mayor of Norwich in 1805, and he used his office to persuade the corporation to plant lots of trees. Hence afterwards, years later, Norwich was named 'The City of Trees.'

Being accoucheur consultant at the hospital did not prevent him from doing his homework. He fathered twelve children, the last four being born at one birth, in 1817, when he was seventy and his wife forty. As a reward for this feat, Norwich Corporation presented him with a piece of silver plate. However, the quads lived only twelve weeks. He was a man who believed that what one has done once, one can do again. Accordingly he read up all the information he could obtain regarding the Hebrew prescription of the tonic Jacob used so that Leah could spend her time in raising stock instead of working in the fields. Although he failed to father more children after the quads, one must give him credit for the fact, that, by using the juice of the mandrake root as a go-getter, he laid the foundation for chemists to work, so that 150 years later, doctors were prescribing to childless wives, what is now known as the fertility pill.

W. H. Barrett and R. P. Garrod, *East Anglian Folklore*, 1976

Biting the bullet

Doctor Messenger Monsey's celebrity owed very little to his wild and prolific pen. His reputation was founded on his conversation and on his habits. He never said anything commonplace; he never did anything in a normal manner. When one of his teeth ached, he would tie it by a length of catgut to a perforated bullet and fire the bullet from a pistol; and this method of dentistry, which he affirmed to be painless, he urged all his friends to adopt. When he went into the country, he was in the habit of putting all his banknotes into the fireplace for safety, carefully hidden under sticks and coal; and on one occasion he returned unexpectedly to find his housekeeper giving a tea-party in his rooms, and the fire blazing merrily.

His talk was vigorous and incessant, anecdotal, highly-flavoured, and crowded (like his letters) with classical quotations and deplorable puns. If it was possible to *smoke* one of the company, he did so without mercy; for he prided himself on his rough sincerity, and exercised a venomous hatred of vanity and affectation.

R. W. Ketton-Cremer, *Norfolk Portraits*, 1944

Wolf-Charlie

He is called Wolf-Charlie, I suppose, by reason of the famished look in his melancholy eyes, of the way in which the skin of his lips, drawn tightly over his gums, exposes his great yellow teeth; by reason of the leanness of his flanks, the shaggy, unkempt hair about his head and face, the half fierce, half frightened expression. He is what is called in employers' parlance 'a three-quarter man,' receiving only three-fourths of the wages of the other labourers.

He has the use of his hands and feet; he is not a 'down fool' like 'Silly Solomon', idiot par excellence of the parish, nor a cripple like Dan'l Luck, whose leg the Runwich Hospital authorities deemed it wise to leave dangling from his trunk after his accident, the foot turned the wrong way, so that for the honour of swinging the useless member he has to go on crutches for all his life. Wolf-Charlie is not specially afflicted in any fashion, yet he is in some indefinable way deficient. His fellow-labourers will not 'du' a harvest with him, and no farmer dares employ him to feed his cattle or to plough or drill.

Yet such labour as is entrusted to him he does with unfailing industry and a dogged, dull persistence. When the vapours hang white and ghost-like over the low-lying meadows, he stands all the day knee-deep in water 'ditching'; and he can always be trusted to 'top and tail' the turnips. In the winter, when work on the farm is only to be obtained by the best men, and such hangers-on as Wolf-Charlie are invariably among the first to be paid off, he sits patiently by the wayside breaking the stones of the road; or for a few pence he will trudge the seven miles to Runwich to fetch a sick neighbour's medicine.

His clothes are in rags, showing the poor flesh in many places which custom and comfort have ordained shall be hidden from view; his thin hairy chest is oftener bare than covered; of Sunday clothes he has none. When he sits on the long dank grass of the roadside bank, with his back to the wind and his shoulders pulled to his ears for warmth, and feels in the red and white bundle beside him for the midday meal which is to support him till he can look for his bowl of potatoes at night, he finds nothing but dry bread there. He does not even possess the 'shut-knife' with which etiquette ordains the agricultural labourer shall carve his al fresco feast, but he pulls it to pieces, wolf-like, with claws and teeth, looking out with the fierce, yet melancholy gaze over the grey and shivering meadows as he drearily chews his food.

Mary Mann, *The Fields of Dulditch*, 1902

The balancing act

A big, bearded man called Barrett, who always wore a peaked cap like a ship's officer's, used to come regularly to Magdalen when I was a boy, selling tapes, buttons, reels of cotton and men's shirts, socks and other garments. He set out each day from his home in King's Lynn and visited, in turn, all the villages round about. His goods were packed into a big wicker hamper which he carried balanced on his head as he walked along with his hands in his pockets. When full that hamper must have weighed four or five stone, and when he came down our way he would have walked at least fourteen miles by the time he got back to Lynn.

My mother often bought things from him. Then he arrived one morning when she was busy with the washing – and she had piles of that to do as we were such a big family. Barrett pounded so hard on the door that the noise, and his loud shout of 'Are ya at hoom?' woke up the baby and made him start to yell and so flustered Mother that she gave the pedlar a good ticking off and told him not to call again.

Arthur Randell, *Fenland Memories*, 1969

The Reeve

Hot-tempered was the Reeve and very thin,
No beard showed on his closely shaven chin.
Above his ears his hair abruptly stopped
And like a priest's his top was neatly cropped.
His legs were long and so extremely lean
They looked like sticks; no calf was to be seen.
His granaries and bins were kept with care;
No auditor could find an error there.
From observation of the drought and rain
He knew the likely yield of seed and grain.
His master's livestock, rams and ewes and cows
His bulls and bullocks, horses, chickens, sows
Were wholly under this Reeve's management.
He'd kept the books, under his covenant,
Since his young lord was in his twentieth year.
No man could ever catch him in arrear.
No bailiff, herdsman, serf or dairymaid
Could fool him with the devious tricks they played.
Feared like the plague was he by common folk.
His lovely house sat on a heath where oak
And ash and maple shade the verdant pasture.
At business he was better than his master.
He had a pile locked in his private coffers
And he could please his lord with subtle offers
Of helpful loans, and with this careful payment
He'd earn his thanks and even handsome raiment.
In youth he'd learned the useful trade and skill
Of carpentry, and he was expert still.
A horse called Scot bore this old Reeve along,
All dappled grey, a big and handsome stallion.
He wore a long surcoat of bluish shade
And by his side he wore a rusty blade.
From Norfolk was this Reeve of which I tell:
He lived close by a town called Baldeswell.
He tucked up like a friar his coat of blue
And he was ever hindmost of our crew.

Geoffrey Chaucer, *Canterbury Tales*

'Mad' Windham's run

One of Norfolk's most notorious 19th century eccentrics was William Frederick Windham of Felbrigg Hall. This splendid mansion, which was the home of the Windham family for centuries, is situated on the eastern most extremity of a high tract of land south-west of Cromer. Just over 100 years ago it was surrounded by over 600 acres of beautifully wooded parkland and was considered one of the finest 'seats' in the county. The Rt. Hon. William Windham, one time friend of Dr Johnson and secretary-at-war under William Pitt during the Napoleonic wars, was the last 'true' Windham to live here. He died in 1810 without issue and the Felbrigg estates were inherited by the grandson of his mother by her first marriage, Admiral Lutin. The Admiral, who eventually assumed the name of Windham, was succeeded by his son William Howe Windham, father of the notorious William Frederick.

The short and stormy life story of this member of a family that bore the name but not the blood of the time honoured Windhams, hit newspaper headlines far beyond the county's boundaries. He inherited the Felbrigg estates when he came of age in 1861, and was to eventually receive from this and other properties an annual income of £9,000. But members of the Windham family considered the new squire's behaviour so strange that they presented on 22nd November, 1861 a petition to the Lords Justices Court, Lincoln's Inn, praying that a writ 'de lunatic inquirendo' be issued against him. After hearing affidavits from either side, the judge considered that a 'prima facie' case had been made out and the resultant Commission under the presidency of Samuel Warren Q.C. held its first sitting on December 16th, 1861.

It was alleged that Windham had married a woman of loose character and had bestowed £1,400 worth of jewellery and an £800 annuity upon her; sold in a wild and reckless manner the ornamental and useful timber on the Felbrigg estate; and was generally incapable of managing his own affairs. Many of Britain's leading lawyers were engaged on the case and the proceedings, which lasted for over a month, were estimated to have cost £160 an hour. Immediately the jury announced the verdict – 'That the said William Frederick Windham, at the time of taking this inquisition, was a person of sound mind so as to be sufficient for the government of himself, his manners, his messuages, his lands, his tenements, his goods and his chattels' – loud cheering broke out in court and outside he was mobbed to his cab.

But the £20,000 costs demanded by the legal profession marked the beginning of the end of Windham's fortune. Within five years he had completely dissipated the residue of this estate and was forced to take up residence at Norwich's Norfolk Hotel. His life of debauchery, which was centred in the more disreputable Norwich taverns, soon earned for him a notoriety that spread far beyond the confines of the city.

He squandered his remaining finances with such reckless extravagance that he was eventually forced to find some form of employment. He started a Norwich–Cromer coach run and very soon became the terror of many travellers on that route. Walter Wicks wrote in his book *Taverns of Old Norwich* that a person who journeyed with 'Mad' Windham was as mad as Windham himself. He continued:

'Nor could a passenger be sure of reaching his destination. 'Mad' Windham might decide, on the spur of the moment. to go to Yarmouth instead of Cromer, by way of a change, leaving the traveller to get to his journey's end the best way he could.'

Passengers recounted of how his horses were invariably urged to gallop no matter how rough the road, while his stentorian voice was frequently heard bellowing in colourful language at any person daring to cross his path. Not surprisingly, his business soon failed, as did the 'Express Coach Company' a few months after he had been engaged as a driver at £1 a week. After many vicissitudes, he was taken ill in his tiny room in the Norfolk Hotel on 31st January, 1866, and died a few days later. He was buried in the family vault at Felbrigg, his only mourners being an old coachman named Tom Saul and a few of his cronies from the Norwich taverns.

R. E. Pestell, 'Norfolk Eccentrics', *Norfolk Fair*, 1968

Yarmouth yarn

He was a large fat man in his middle fifties, more square than round, with small eyes, a florid complexion and, when he was amused, a deep hearty chuckle which would pour from his thick flabby throat. He always wore a long black overcoat much-stained with remains of food eaten long ago, a huge trilby hat perched on his head, and tattered trousers hanging over grimy boots.

'Hello, matey, no work yet?' I would enquire.

'I might get a start tomorrow,' he would usually say.

Now this old chap wasn't lazy but he just wasn't suited to work. It was such a pity for he was quite a likeable fellow. He'd been on the Labour Exchange since it was a Nissen Hut.

One wag told me the reason why he couldn't find work was that he was registered as a pearl diver. He could start work right away if pearls were being found in Breydon Water. His daily food intake was mostly odd snacks here and there where he could cadge them and his capacity for food was phenomenal. So was his ability for 'cadging'. Mine was not the only food establishment where a broad hint could attract a bacon roll.

He was dirty and greedy and a social misfit but he had one remarkable attribute: a good voice. Sometimes in the quiet periods of business I'd pull out the old guitar and we'd both go into a rendering of 'Hello Dolly' or something of the kind. He knew all the words of most of the pre-war songs. That, and the fact that he never used bad language, made me very tolerant towards him

It's quite some while now since he left the town, but for a generation or more I am sure he will be remembered amongst people when they gather together reminiscing upon the old Yarmouth, a way of life coming to a close. I remember him well, harking back to that cold wet November morning standing there with a smile on his face and, on the end of his nose, a dewdrop glistening like a new born pearl.

Jimmy O'Connor, *Memories of a Market Trader*, 1984

Scientific King

Years ago Rockland was the home and kingdom of that remarkable old broadsman, the late 'Scientific' Fuller, the self-
styled and universally accepted 'King of Rockland Broad'. Like
the late Charlie Gibbs at Surlingham, he stoutly upheld the
public right to shoot and fish unhindered on Rockland Broad
which, the broad being tidal, is a right unchallengable.

'Scientific' lived in an old houseboat on the broad. There he
dwelt with his gun-punt and his great muzzle-loading punt-
gun, his shoulder-guns and bow-nets, his eel spears and his
dog. Short and broad-shouldered, with a great barrel of a chest,
'stuggy', as they say in Norfolk, his eyes gleamed fiercely from
a great black bush of beard, whiskers and unkempt hair. He
feared neither man nor devil, and he was a master fisherman,
a crack shot.

'Scientific' could skate at full speed across the broad, with
his gun in his hand, suddenly throw the gun to his shoulder
and shoot, stone-dead, a gull wheeling and swooping overhead.

He caught an immense number of fish, shot thousands of
wild-fowl and, in his time, collected many rare birds for wealthy
collectors when such reprehensible practices were winked at. I
shudder to think how many bitterns, bearded tits, harriers, rare
warblers and uncommon ducks went into the bloodstained,
canvas 'side-bag' which swung on a broad strap from his
shoulders.

This uncouth, lovable, pugnacious old man would swallow
incredible quantities of beer at the inn at the head of Rockland
Dyke, and then, rattling his hob-nailed, leather water-boots on
the stone floor, he would dance a wild jig which struck sparks
from the flags and end up by challenging any man there to
fight him for a quart. None did unless they were very young
or very drunk.

In winter, when the punt-guns boomed through snowy mist
far away on the tidal flats at Breydon Water, 'Scientific' would
be afloat in his little, low, grey-painted duck-punt, the great
muzzle-loader, with a barrel 6 feet long, lying flat and menac-
ing in its cradle. A few minutes after the booming echoes

sounded from Breydon, teams of duck and wigeon with some-times skeins of grey geese would whistle overhead and plunge in sheets of foam on to the surface of the broad.

Like a shadow the old man's punt crept silently out of its little bay among the reeds and floated flat and ghostly towards the resting fowl. Foot by foot he spritted or paddled silently forward. Then the trigger was pulled. There came a red, sear-ing flame, a foot long, from the muzzle, a billowing cloud of grey smoke, a thudding boom that echoed across the lonely fen and, in a frenzy of wings, the fowl were up and away, skirling with fright. On the water floated a dozen, perhaps a score, of dead and wounded. That was the old man's living in winter.

In summer he caught and netted fish, speared eels and took them in his great funnel-shaped 'grigs' woven by hand from thin osiers.

If anyone poached on 'Scientific's' preserves, he would shoot at them as soon as look at them. Yet he was universally loved, a sort of uncouth cross between 'Bloody Morgan' and Thoreau. When he died half Norfolk mourned him and men of science who had enjoyed his company and bought his rare specimens knew that a last link with the primitive race of broadsmen had gone for ever.

James Wentworth Day, East Anglian Magazine, 1976

Best in the business

It's an interesting job being a nightsoil man. True, you don't really get to meet people much, and when you do they tend to keep their distance, but you have the world to yourself as you go from house to house, emptying their privies while they sleep.

The Sheringham nightsoil man was Lawrence Littlejohn and he was proud of the job that he did. He was a fully paid-up member of the Nightsoil Association, but he was more ambitious than that. He considered that when it came to excrement excavation, he was the best operative in the business.

Not that there was any competition in Sheringham. Not any more. He'd seen them all off with his quality of service, his speed of response and just a few old-fashioned threats. The last of them had been a keen gardener who had given up when he found the severed head of his favourite horse-radish in his bed. Well, business is business. If you can't stand the heat, get out of the kitchen. Either that or open the window for a bit.

So now Lawrence had the field to himself. 'I'm Lord of all I behold,' he thought, as he looked to see if his bucket was full yet. 'What I have I own,' he mused, as he trundled his loaded cart down the street. And sometimes you saw interesting things of the night. True, you smelled a lot of interesting things as well, but you soon got used to that.

Tonight, it was quiet. Of course, it had been noisy earlier. There had been big celebrations when the crews got home because there was a definite sense that Sheringham was winning the war. They'd toured the streets singing 'Four–two, four–two' on and on to a mindless tune. (You have to suspect that it would have been exactly the same in Cromer, if they hadn't all been out with torches searching for Cromeo. Except that probably wouldn't have been singing 'Two–four' with quite such enthusiasm.)

Chris Sugden and Sid Kipper, *Crab Wars*, 1999

Norfolk witchcraft

A short time ago I was conversing with a tenant-farmer in mid-Norfolk about things in general, and, steering gradually towards the subject in which just then I was particularly interested, I asked him whether he believed in ghosts or witchcraft. It made him look as serious as if I had questioned him concerning eternal torments or bodily resurrection.

'Well,' says he, 'there ain't no manner o' doubt about ghosts, anyhow, 'cause, though I never saw one, I felt one. I was once coming through that there plantation yonder one dark night, and as true as I'm alive a ghost laid his hand on my shoulder, and I felt it cold against my face. As for witches I aren't a-going to say for certain, 'cause I don't know; but the Bible tells us about 'em, and we ought to believe that. There's a young chap in the village what got married a couple o' years ago, and his mother-in-law lived with him. She was so continually nagging and grumbling that he couldnít stand it no longer. So he told everybody he was a-going to Norwich to consult the witch; and when he come back he said as how she promised to do pretty warm for *somebody* if she didn't mind her p's and q's. Whether 'twas the witch or whether she was frightened I can't say, but that there mother-in-law didn't carry on none o' her pranks arter that.' Then he hook his shaggy head and sighed, as much as to say, 'If I had to vote one way or t'other, I should vote on witchcraft.'

Charles Roper, *Where The Birds Sing*, 1894

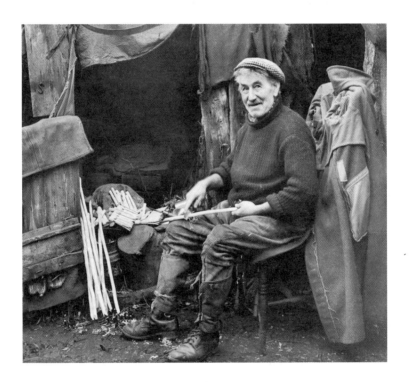

CRAFTSMAN CHARACTER – *making linen pegs from ashwood was one of the pastimes of John Harris of Whissonsett, known to his close friends as 'Old Cardy'. This picture was taken in 1953.*

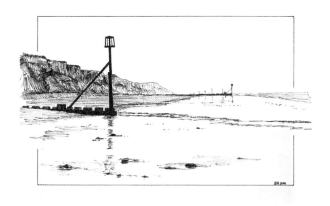

ALONG THE COAST

The Norfolk coastline, a benign playground for so many in summer, needs little goading to bare its battleground teeth. Erosion continues to gnaw away like a giant rogue coypu, while scientific experts issue dire warnings about global warming and the need for coastal defence work running into millions of pounds to protect against rising sea levels. Dramatic losses and hideous damage have been too regular throughout history to ignore such admonitions.

In an article entitled 'The Hungry Sea', penned for the Eastern Daily Press *in April 1952, Jonathan Mardle (pseudonym of Eric Fowler, the paper's leader writer and celebrated essayist) concluded with awful foresight: 'The sea is older than science; it recks nothing of time, and it never gives up trying.'*

On January 31st and February 1st, 1953, a great storm surge, accompanied by gale force winds, caused widespread flooding along the East Coast, involving grievous loss of life and extensive damage to property. In total, 307 people died, 32,000 had to be evacuated and 24,000 homes were flooded and damaged. Bleak statistics that scarcely do justice to such a savage episode.

An unceasing conflict between land and sea naturally dominates this selection, but there is room for scenes from a burgeoning holiday trade built on the arrival of the railways, more gentle reflections among the hooded crows of Wells and a tribute to one of the bravest lifeboatmen of them all.

The hooded crows

A small, ancient, village-like town, set in a low flat land next the sea, or separated from the sea by a mile-wide marsh, grey in summer, but now rust-brown in its autumnal colour. The fisher-folk are poor, and their harvest consists mainly of shell-fish, mussels, whelks, clams, and they also dig at low water for sand-worms to be sold for bait. They are, as I think I remarked before, like their feathered fellow-creatures, the hooded crows; and indeed they resemble crows when seen, small and black, scattered far out on the wide waste of sand. When the men are away at sea and those noisy little animals, the children, are shut up in school, you can imagine that there is no longer any life in Wells; you would not be in a quieter place on the wide brown marsh itself, nor on the low grassy sand-hills faintly seen in the distance, nor on the wide stretch of sand beyond, where the men, crow-like, are seeking their subsistence.

W. H. Hudson, *Adventures Among Birds*, 1923

Trippers' delights

Yarmouth, the paradise of excursionists, who are poured in here by the thousands in the glorious summer weather, is, too, as strange as its surroundings. One scarcely knows how to take it, so to say, whether to look upon it as the haunt pure and simple of the cheap 'tripper,' or to regard it as a charming, quaint old seaport, picturesque in the highest degree, interesting from end to end; a place wherein to study the old 'salt' in his native lair, or to take 'impressions' of the East-end holiday-maker in his most festive mood. A single impression of Yarmouth would be little better than a blur; a wild confused jumble of shipping, crowds, sands, barrel-organs, eating-saloons, and public-houses; noise, vulgarity, perpetual movement, and vivid colouring. Whereas Yarmouth to be thoroughly appreciated must be seen in detail. Thousands of those who come here annually know nothing of this fine old town, save that it has a magnificent extent of beach – the scene of wild orgies on the part of excited excursionists – that refreshments and ships, greasy paper-bags and lodgings are abundant, and all the advantages of the Old Kent Road are pleasantly combined with those of a seaside resort of peculiar excellence. They come to 'enjoy' themselves, and for that purpose they hie them to the shining sands, wherein they dig holes and deposit their many babies, duly provided with feeding bottles; while they themselves, fortified at the frequent and conveniently-adjacent saloons, dance to the strains of piano-organs, cornets, and various other musical instruments. Of its 'sights' they know nothing, when the Aquarium, the Nelson column, the Market-place, the pier and, maybe, the race-course have been excepted. These they can scarcely help seeing, for the pier in the holiday season is certainly not a sight to be overlooked, and the Nelson monument is visible to the naked eye for miles around. Moreover, the unfortunate, long-suffering donkeys, and poor, broken-kneed ponies that afford the excursionist such exquisite enjoyment, can be sometimes induced to go so far as this fine memorial of the great naval victor along the beautiful Marine Parade and Drive, the West-end of Yarmouth.

Annie Berlyn, *Sunrise-Land*, 1894

Peggotty's abode

Ham carrying me on his back and a small box of ours under his arm, and Peggotty carrying another small box of ours, we turned down lanes bestrewn with bits of chips and little hill-ocks of sand, and went past gasworks, ropeworks, boat-build-ers' yards, shipwrights' yards, ship-breakers' yards, caulkers' yards, riggers' lofts, smiths' forges, and a great litter of such places, until we came out upon the dull waste I had already seen at a distance; when Ham said, 'Yon's our house, Mas'r Davy!'

I looked in all directions, as far as I could stare over the wilderness, and away at the sea, and away at the river, but no house could *I* make out. There was a black barge, or some other kind of superannuated boat, not far off, high and dry on the ground, with an iron funnel sticking out of it for a chimney and smoking very cosily; but nothing else in the way of a habitation that was visible to *me*.

'That's not it,' said I - 'that ship-looking thing?'

'That's it, Mas'r Davy,' returned Ham.

If it had been Aladdin's palace, roc's egg and all, I suppose I could not have been more charmed with the romantic idea of living in it. There was a delightful door cut in the side, and it was roofed in, and there were little windows in it; but the wonderful charm of it was, that it was a real boat, which had no doubt been upon the water hundreds of times, and which had never been intended to be lived in, on dry land. That was the captivation of it to me. If it had ever been meant to be lived in, I might have thought it small, or inconvenient, or lonely; but never having been designed for any such use, it became a perfect abode.

Charles Dickens, *David Copperfield*, 1850

From Yarmouth Sands

The beacon's answer from th' exploding deck,
Summons all hands, to aid th' impending wreck;
And not in vain; the bravest of the brave
Propel a yawl undaunted t'ward the wave.
Yet, though from fear or lingering doubt exempt,
It proves an arduous, hazardous, attempt.
United efforts are requir'd to push
The ponderous boat; together on they rush,
Till, buoyant on th' uplifting surge, they pass
In triumph through the dashing, trembling mass
Of mingling waves high rising o'er their head,
Midst spray, and foam, and sand, wide scattered.
Loud cheers ascending from the anxious throng,
Proclaim their courage, and their praise prolong;
Onward they go, conceal'd, reveal'd, again
They dive beneath the mountains of the main;

Once more their sail is visible, but with slope
That proves the blast, and almost palsies hope;
Can they yet dare with the fierce storm to cope?
They right again, one fortunate effort more –
Breathless emotion pants along the shore;
On tower, and cliff, the jetty, and the pier,
Flutters the wish, or agitates the fear;
A pause of horror sinks the heart of all.
The boat is swamp'd; a huge sea in its fall
Tremendous, from its rolling giant height,
For ever has envelop'd it from sight!
And 'whelm'd with its precipitated weight.
Vessel, and gallant crew – consign'd to fate.

> By a Southtown Resident 1852, in *East Anglian Verse*,
> Goodwyn, E. A., and Baxter, J. C. (eds), 1974

Older than science

Nowadays, of course, we live in the age of reinforced concrete and national organisation. Coastal towns and villages are no longer left to fight, alone, their battle against the sea. There are protection schemes all up an down the coast, until you may wonder whether the eventual answer to erosion will be a concrete wall from Cley to Orford Ness, to take the place of the solid rock that Nature failed to supply. Yet walls alone are not enough. Sooner or later the sea will always get underneath or round a wall even as when in play you try to dam a pool on the beach, and strengthen the dam with the biggest pebbles you can find, the tide laps in, and turns the sand beneath the pebbles into ooze and there is no more dam. Sea walls are only a reinforcement of the real defence, which is the inconstant beach, and the device of the engineer is by the cunning situation of groynes to induce the sea, instead of scouring away the sand, to pile up a beach against itself.

Or he can set the wind to work for him - place faggots, plant marram grass, and perhaps eventually pine trees, above the tide mark, and leave the wind to pile sand higher and higher about these obstacles until it builds a rampart of dunes held together by the roots of the grass or the trees. Which is why any thoughtless holiday-maker who makes a slide down a sand dune deserves to have his fool hindquarters lacerated by a buried thorn faggot. It is a little hint that the dunes are there for a purpose, and not for fun.

But with all these precautions, security is only bought with constant vigilance and continual reinforcement of the defences. The sea is older than science; it recks nothing of time, and it never gives up trying.

> Jonathan Mardle, 'The Hungry Sea: April 1952' in *The Best of Jonathan Mardle, Volume One*, 1982

Swallowed by sea

Last Rilings shut the door behind him, and it took some force to do it against the resistance of the gale which sought to come in with him. He took off his battered cap to shake the wetness from it, as if to convince old Martha that nothing was bad enough to really rattle him. But then he moved urgently to the bed from which his now-invalid wife looked up at him.

'How are things, Last?' she asked.

The old man looked down at her, deep into the tired old eyes. For fifty years they had been partners through rough and smooth, and there had been more of the rough than the other. It had not been an easy path, but it had been made less difficult by the help each received from the other and the knowledge of the partner's devotion. She depended on him now, and, by God, he would not fail her. Yet he could not hide the seriousness of the situation from her. She would know if he lied, and, anyway, she would want to know the truth. She had to know the truth, for something extra would be demanded of her tired old frame tonight.

'Not so good, Martha,' he told her. 'The sea is right up the sandhills and the tide's not full yet. I fear something terrible is going to happen tonight, The waves are like mountains, girl.'

'What are you going to do about it?'

'We can either get out or move upstairs.'

'Out?' said Martha, incredulously. 'You're not taking me out on a night like this. And where do you think we would go if we did go out?'

'I don't know,' said her husband, 'but we'd find somewhere. Someone would take us in further inland.'

'And how far inland do you think you'd take me, the state I'm in?'

He gave her a smile, poor old soul, and she returned it. On each side it carried an expression of the love that had grown and blossomed over half a century or more.

'I'll move you upstairs, Martha,' said Last. 'Then I'll take some stuff up out of the pantry. I don't know how long we'll be up there, but we don't want to be hungry, do we?'

Again, the old woman smiled.

'Don't forget the stout,' she reminded him. 'I couldn't stay up there without my stout.'

And that was the last that Martha Rilings ever said to her husband. He thought about that afterwards. 'Don't forget my stout.' She never drank that stout. It was swallowed by the sea.

Peter Bagshaw, *The Gap In The Dunes*, 1959

Shattered walls

Deep floods penetrated up the Wiveton valley. At Overstrand much of the already precarious walling and parade were badly damaged; the mass-concrete walls were shattered and portions overturned. At Mundesley the sea-wall was undermined at its eastern end, and waves were smashing up the concrete promenade as though it were so much hardboard. The uncompleted sea-wall at Walcott was battered and outflanked; the sea attacked the clay cliffs at the rear, washing away part of the coast road. The main street of Walcott was destroyed and many buildings wrecked. At Palling the waves burst through the trampled gap in the dunes about 8 p.m., engulfed all the buildings at the seaward end of the village and swept thousands of tons of sand up the village street, to lie there afterwards in drifts 5ft. deep. Seven people were drowned. On both sides of Sea Palling, at Eccles and Horsey, the concrete sea-walls were very heavily pounded. The waves overtopped them and cut away the dunes behind. At Eccles the wall collapsed over a length of about one and a half miles.

Further along the coast Great Yarmouth was virtually isolated after floodwater had severed all main lines of communication. Here the Cobholm and Southtown areas were badly affected for, besides the overflowing river Yare, they had to contend with floods from behind when the Breydon wall collapsed and tons of water came surging across the marshes, through gaps in the railway embankment and into the streets.

Dorothy Summers, *The East Coast Floods*, 1978

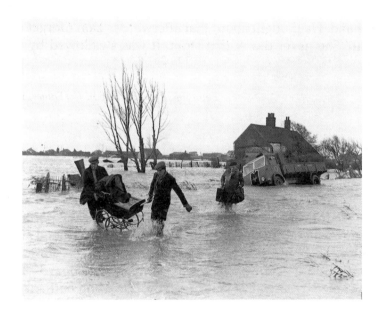

Floods at Snettisham: 1953

On a Friend's Escape from Drowning off the Norfolk Coast

Came up that cold sea at Cromer like a running grave
  Beside him as he struck
Wildly towards the shore, but the blackcapped wave
  Crossed him and swung him back,
And he saw his son digging in the castled dirt that could save.
  Then the farewell rock
Rose a last time to his eyes. As he cried out
  A pawing gag of the sea
Smothered his cry and he sank in his own shout
  Like a dying airman. Then she
Deep near her son asleep on the hourglass sand
  Was awakened by whom
Save the Fate who knew that this was the wrong time:
  And opened her eyes
On the death of her son's begetter. Up she flies
  Into the hydra-headed
Grave as he closes his life upon her who for
  Life has so richly bedded him.
But she drove through his drowning like Orpheus and tore
  Back by the hair
Her escaping bridegroom. And on the sand their son
  Stood laughing where
He was almost an orphan. Then the three lay down
  On that cold sand,
Each holding the other by a living hand.

George Barker in *Norfolk (Poet's England series)*, 1994

Farewell to hero

The hearse, the family mourners, and fifteen official cars
followed the band of fishermen. Mr Kelly Harrison, bowman
of the lifeboat, carried Blogg's twelve decorations on a black-
velvet cushion. A lorry carried a hundred wreaths - a riot of
summer's colour in the midst of navy-blue and black.

The procession formed, and moved past the west-door of
the church, along High Street, and New Street; past the spot

where Henry Blogg was born, and within a few yards of the cliff-top, where he had stood so many times scanning the sky and gauging the weather. The route was deeply lined by people who watched silently as the cortège turned into Prince of Wales Road and inland along the Holt Road.

On the outskirts of the town the fishermen fell into two ranks on either side of the road, allowing the hearse and mourners to pass on their long journey to the new cemetery, nearly two miles out of town. Then they got into a coach, and, by making a detour, arrived at the gates before the procession and lined the main entrance.

There, on the high ground, in one of the loveliest parts of Norfolk, overlooking the heath and wood and the distant sea, they laid Henry Blogg. The seaman was home from the sea.

They left him there, and the man who never had a garden was now covered by costly flowers. Away from the sea's moaning and the gulls' screaming, he lies buried beside his wife Ann and his daughter 'Queenie'. A simple, grey mottled kerb and headstone enclose the spot bearing the short name, the strong name, the unforgettable name – Henry Blogg.

Cyril Jolly, *Henry Blogg of Cromer*, 1958

'Degraded creatures'

A fortnight ago we drew attention to the want that existed on the part of some of the bathers at Cromer of that sense of decency and self respect which is supposed to be innate in civilised human beings. We are sorry it is necessary to refer to the subject again, for we trusted that the warning then given would be sufficient to let offenders know that this violation of the unwritten laws of decency would not be tolerated at this watering place. Unfortunately, the nuisance has not yet been stopped, and we have been urged both by visitors and residents to raise a protest against the bathing of men and women within the same area. Those degraded creatures who have no sense of propriety in this respect will have to take their lessons from beachmen, or seek a beach unfrequented by persons worthy of being described as ladies and gentlemen. Sometimes whole families will enter a bathing machine, regardless of the fact that it is in the midst of the ladies' ground, and there both sexes will go through their natatory exercises, to the disgust of those who have hired the surrounding machines. The space between the two sets of bathing machines is too narrow, and this is taken advantage of by some of the lowest class of bathers, who will swim into the part set apart for the other sex. One gentleman who complained to us of the indecencies described the clothing of some of these men as scant in the extreme, but some fishermen have told us of cases in which men with female companions have engaged a boatman to row them about parallel with the beach, and have then stripped themselves of every shred of clothing and entered the water in a state of complete nudity. If there be any who lightly regard this demoralising conduct, and consider it beneath notice, they may ask how it is that the beachmen should give vent to expressions of shame about it. The reason is not only that poor fishermen have a code of honour, but that they know quite well the tendency of this conduct is to drive respectable visitors from Cromer. The town has gained a wide popularity as a resort of refined society, and to this its rapid growth is due; but if its character is to be spoilt by the miserable dregs of society, it will quite as rapidly decline. As a boat owner remarked to us, these creatures should be hooted on their return to the beach.

from *The Cromer and North Walsham Post*, 23 August, 1890 in Andy Reid (ed.), *Cromer and Sheringham, the Growth of the Holiday Trade, 1877 - 1914*

Royal cigar

The Le Strange family of Hunstanton Hall lived just inland of what came to be called Old Hunstanton and decided to exploit the growing demand for seaside holidays by turning Hunstanton St Edmund, on the low cliffs at the angle of the Wash and the long sweep of the Norfolk coast, into New Hunstanton. The key to this was the arrival of the railway, after an almost straight run from London through Cambridge and

Ely, in 1862. Three years later a church was built, followed by a pier, followed by a whole town, much of it designed by William Butterfield and built in the soft ginger carrstone of the region.

With its magnificent beach of hard sand and striped chalk and carrstone cliffs, New Hunstanton became fashionable not only for genteel holidays, but for preparatory schools and the infra-structure needed by visiting middle-class parents, notably the Sandringham Hotel. 'A compact little watering-place with everything on a miniature scale – a little railway station, six or seven bathing machines, etc.', wrote a visiting Norfolk clergyman (Rev. Benjamin Armstrong of East Dereham) in his diary in 1864, then noting that the royal seal of approval had been bestowed by the future King Edward VII on excursions from his newly-acquired country house in Sandringham. 'The most curious thing about this place is the celebrated cliff, so full of interest to the geologist. Here it is that the Prince and Princess of Wales are in the habit of taking luncheon, a servant laying the cloth on one of the rocks, while the future King of England sits on another, smoking his cigar.'

Tom Pocock, *Norfolk, Pimlico County History Guides*, 1995

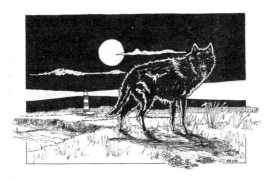

TWISTS IN THE TALE

Norfolk has long been a fertile source of inspiration for those who like to dip their pens in a drop of mystery, a favourite hideout for shifty strangers and brazen beasts with mayhem and murder in mind.

Perhaps Sherlock Holmes helped put the rural idyll in perspective when he pronounced in The Copper Beeches: 'It is my belief, Watson, founded upon my experience, that the lowest and vilest alleys in London do not present a more dreadful record of sin than does the smiling and beautiful countryside.'

More recently crime queen P. D. James underlined how a charming and tranquil setting can provide that contrast which enhances terror, parodying Rupert Brooke to ask:

'Stands the church clock at ten to three?
And is there arsenic still for tea?'

Witches, legends, ghosts, hauntings and things that defy any logical explanation all go into the pot to stir the plot – with old Shuck straining at the leash for another run while it bubbles.

Scorching breath

Not a sound broke the silence as I waited there by the edge of a pool which gleamed like silver in the moonlight. One by one the lights from the distant village faded and presently the shouts and laughter of the merrymakers at Wells died away on the breeze. Then there settled down a grim stillness which seemed pregnant with menace and I clasped my stick the tighter as I realized my absolute loneliness...

After what seemed a long interval, a gentle sighing came from away by the seashore, some two or three miles off, and the moonlight grew steadily brighter. Then, as I watched from the cover of my hollow, I saw an indefinable shadow, far away on the horizon. The eerie silence was rent by the most appalling howl to which I have ever listened – it froze the blood in my veins and caused my hair to stand right on end. And the shadow was coming nearer. Believe me or not, as you will, it may have all been imagination or the result of the tales I had previously heard; but I saw that black hound as clearly as I shall ever see anything again...

With a yell of terror I jumped from the hollow and fled. Not once did I look behind, but I felt that the creature was in pursuit. Never had I run as I ran that night. Stumbling, cursing, breathing heavily, I tore up the lane and at last gained the threshold of the cottage. With a profound feeling of thankfulness I knocked upon the door and called to the cottager to open. In a moment a light appeared above and footsteps descended and came along the passage. Then I heard a welcome voice – 'Do yew not be jiffling, sir, I be a-coming.'

And as the bolt was undone and the key turned I glanced around to see a pair of ferocious eyes fixed upon me and to feel on my neck a scorching breath. The hound was actually about to spring as the door opened and I fell fainting into the arms of my host. One look he gave and then shut the door with a bang as a great black body seemed to leap through the air, and come thudding on the ground outside ...

On the following morning I told the full story and heard only the comment. 'Yew be a durned fool and lucky to escape at that.'

Christopher Marlowe, *People and Places in Marshland*, 1927

The Shuck

Panting, plodding, panting,
Plodding, plodding along.
With his tangled hair that sweeps the ground,
And a haunting, sobbing, gasping sound,
For ever he's plodding on ...

When the night wind howls round the chimney cowls,
And the rain beats on the pane,
And a ghostly moon lights the racing clouds
As they hurry across the sky like shrouds,
Then the worried hound in the farmyard howls -
    For it's coming down the lane!

There's a lull in the breeze through the dripping trees,
For a moment all is still.
Then a shadowy shape comes out of the night,
And it passes by, and is gone from sight ...
Like a sigh of relief returns the breeze,
And follows it over the hill.

Through the Norfolk lanes, in the Wintry rain,
It moves, and leaves no mark;
And many will start from their sleep in fright
At the thought of the thing that comes in the night,
And those who see it will think again,
Ere they wander after dark ....

    Panting, plodding. panting.
    Plodding, plodding along,
    With his tangled hair that sweeps the ground,
    And a haunting, sobbing, gasping sound,
    For ever he's plodding on ....

John Kett, *Remembered in Rhyme*, 1957

127

Powerful sword

Long ago there was a strange belief which caused pilgrims to hurry to the Norfolk village of Winfarthing and the husbands of the neighbourhood to carefully check their chandler's bills. It was all because of the curious properties attributed to the Good Sword of Winfarthing which was said to have belonged to a felon who had claimed sanctuary in the village church.

When the robber departed, he left his sword behind to become the object of 'vow makings, crouchinges and kissenges' by people from far and near. Some came because the sword was believed to assist in finding lost goods, particularly stolen or strayed horses. But it was when a wife set a candle before Winfarthing's sword Sunday after Sunday that a husband had reason to be alarmed. It might indicate that she was remarkably forgetful but it could be the signal that she wanted to be rid of her lord and master, because the sword was believed to have the power to shorten a man's life. To gain the help of the sword's powers to end a marriage, a wife had to burn a candle before it each and every Sunday for a year. One wonders how many marital arguments were caused by the wives of Winfarthing trotting off to church or husbands meticulously checking on the candle consumption!

An alternative way was to make a gift of a peck of oats to St. Wilgefortis, better known to wives as St. Uncumber, because, it was believed, she could uncumber a good wife of a bad husband by packing him off to the devil on a horse. The mythical saint was said to have been a pagan King of Portugal's daughter who prayed to be made ugly when her father wanted to marry her off. As a result she grew a beard which had the effect of frightening away the suitor and causing her angry father to have her put to death.

Winfarthing's sword has disappeared but St. Uncumber with bearded face can be seen in Worstead church with an-other saint of doubtful background, St. William of Norwich, an alleged victim of ritual murder by Jews like St. Robert of Bury St Edmunds and little St. Hugh of Lincoln.

Peter Jeffery, *East Anglian Ghosts, Legends and Lore*, 1988

Shattered heart

A fascinating and gruesome tale surrounds the origin of the carving of a heart located in the Tuesday Market Place in King's Lynn. This prosperous port had, like so many other European towns, a most horrid way of dealing with certain criminals: boiling to the death. Such displays in Lynn's market place were sure crowd-pullers in 16th century England.

The popularity of boiling to the death reached a peak in 1531 with the introduction of an Act specifically dealing with poisoners and which legalised the use of the cauldron as a means of execution.

That year a maid servant was extremely unfortunate both to have poisoned her mistress and to get caught. She was duly sentenced, though her act may well have been a simple case of food poisoning misunderstood by a superstitious people; nobody now knows.

Taken in chains to the market place, she was suspended above a giant boiling cauldron over an enormous fire. At the very moment that the water boiled, the terrified maid was lowered into the cauldron, raised and lowered again and again, as was the general practice. Amazingly, the water being so scalding, the girl's chest burst open and her heart was propelled across the market place, hitting the wall on the other side. There today, you can see the spot marked with a carving of a heart in a diamond, (on the wall of a house at the narrow end of the market place).

Rick O'Brien, *East Anglian Curiosities*, 1992

Ancient figure

Here was another reputed witch. She died many years ago. When I knew her she lived in a dark house in Cromer Street, and very like a witch she certainly looked – a little feeble woman, with nutcracker nose and chin, usually leaning upon a stick. I don't know any one for whom my childish heart was so much drawn out in pity and compassion.

I remember Uncle Arthur saying he used to visit her when he was curate here; and I believe I am right in saying on one occasion when he took her a piece of pudding she threw it in his face. This I am not sure of, but she was thought very proud.

Louey and I, with some fear and trembling, used to go into her dark room, the windows being tightly closed up – to their shame and disgrace be it spoken – because the boys of the place used to 'bung the witch'.

Oh, our hearts bled for the poor, miserable old woman. It was some moments before our eyes got accustomed to the light, and at last we could discern the ancient figure, with its withered hands stretched out over the embers. She would look up with the words, 'Oh, it's you, Rosy, is it?' – she used to call me 'Rosy' – and she would take what we had brought, and would listen to a few words read by the firelight.

I remember how dazzling it was when we got into the sunlight again, and what a relief we felt it to have got away.

There used to be a large black pot, with three little legs hanging over the fire – a regular witch's cauldron.

At last the sad news came, poor Strutty Cox had been picked up lying dead in her coalhouse, into which the snow was drifting heartlessly.

Poor old woman! Had you looked to the Saviour and seen His smile of reconciliation? We don't know, but it is written, 'God is love!'

Emma Piggott, *East Anglian Reminiscences*, 1890

Dawn chorus

Dawn was breaking across the city. Its cold, bleak light silently probed every hidden corner, melting away every secret shadow that clung between the close-crowded houses. Brick by brick, cobble by cobble it spread, bringing a blaze of colour to the tall fluted windows of the old museum on Elm Hill. It touched and brought life to the knights and prancing horses carved in stark relief on the Watchgate door. The dawn moved on across the narrow alleyways and ruined courtyards, spreading as relentlessly as the tide breaking across a beach of pebbles. It flowed beneath the night-dark archway into Goats Head Alley, to grey the cobbles of that claustrophobic courtyard and wash away the shadows. It painted the new morning across the taxidermist's open doorway.

Ludo Strewth hovered in the courtyard, wringing his hands together helplessly and listening, following the eerie dawn chorus of the animals that barged and stampeded their way past him and into the darkness of his shop. He could hear the two bears howling somewhere in the Narrows.

'You're making enough noise to wake the dead,' he hissed, as their shrieks echoed between the steep weather-bleached roofs all around him.

But there were other sounds that made him anxious, other sounds that broke the dawn silence. The faint wail of police sirens in the direction of the Castle Narrows and the clamour of an ambulance crossing the city, but closer, much closer, somewhere in the vicinity of Elm Hill or Castle Street, he could hear the sound of a car.

'Quickly, I command you to get back to the shop. I command you to do as I say,' he hissed at the shadowy animal forms that suddenly emerged from beneath the archway and streamed all around him towards the open door.

Their unshod hooves and clawed feet echoed in the courtyard, cats hissed and birds flew around his face as Ludo counted the hurrying shapes through the doorway.

'The bears! Where are the bears?' he cried as he realized that the sound of the car he had heard was getting dangerously close. He heard the squeak of brakes and door being thrown open. The car must be just beyond the low archway. Now there were voices and the sound of boots on the uneven cobbles. They were moving towards the courtyard. He retreated back into his shop and securely bolted the door.

Mike Jefferies, *Shadows in the Watchgate*, 1991

Devil's Dyke

According to a local shepherd, the round barrow known as Hangour Hill at Beachamwell was formed by the Devil scraping his spade against a tree after making a 'ditch'. Presumably this was the earthwork known as Devil's Dyke a little to the west of the tumulus.

Was it the Devil's visit to Beachamwell that was recorded in the little thatched church of St Mary in the middle of the village? Here on a pillar in medieval times someone scratched the little picture now known as the 'Beachamwell Demon', a humanoid figure with horns and animal ears, his long tongue sticking out and a tree branch in his hand.

Jennifer Westwood, *Gothick Norfolk*, 1989

Swinging rope

PC 91 Williams had patrolled country beats for over twelve years, and had never during that time encountered anything which could not be explained by factual or physical means. Williams was a practical man, not given to imaginative flights, and believing in what he actually saw rather than in what he was told or what he heard by way of gossip. He was married, living in the local police house about three miles from Didlington Hall, and he was constable to four parishes, the most rural of which was Didlington. It was a hamlet only, a collection of scattered farm cottages, one farm and the village church. Its total population numbered just over eighty persons.

Some ten years previously the owner of Didlington Hall had died and the cemetery in which he was buried lies only a short distance from the Hall.

It was a cold night and Constable Williams found his heavy serge overcoat inadequate to keep out the cutting wind. He glanced at his watch, shining the powerful hand torch on to the dial. The time was 22.50 hours. He calculated that if he cycled slowly he should reach Didlington Church at 23.00 hours, which would complete his last round at Didlington before moving on to another parish for his final tour of duty for that night. It was not a good night to be out in the open. Didlington is a heavily wooded area and the wind whistled between the avenues of trees on either side of the lane.

Williams was about to mount his bicycle when he heard a sound which made him pause. At first he thought it was the noise of the wind through the woodland; then as the sound was repeated he recognized it as that of a clanging bell. It occurred to him that it must be the chiming of the church clock, until he remembered that the church clock had not worked for years; it was stuck permanently at seven o'clock.

He jumped on his bicycle and pedalled in the direction of the church. The bell continued to ring sonorously as he rode, and he counted twenty-five tolls. It was certainly the bell of Didlington church. As he reached the church gate, the ringing abruptly ceased, and the silence which followed it was more alarming than the previous din. There was no sound now apart from the wind in the trees and the snapping of small pieces of decayed wood as the constable moved into the church pathway.

Various possibilities occurred to him as he walked up the path under the overhanging elms. It could be a village joker playing games with him; or children larking with the bell. But not at this hour, and not on a night like this. However, something or someone had caused the half-ton bell to swing and it was his job to investigate the occurrence.

The church door was locked, but he knew the key was usually left under the doormat, and with the aid of his torch he located and fitted it into the lock. He turned the key with care, trying to make as little noise as possible in order not to alert any intruder who might be within.

Having unlocked the door, he swung it open as far as it would go, at the same time flashing on his torch and shining it over the pews, down the nave and under the belfry, where he knew the bell-rope hung. He saw the bell-rope and then felt the hair prickle on his scalp. The bell rope was still swinging; it was as though it had only a moment before been released by whoever was holding it. Yet there was not a soul in sight.

The constable's mouth went dry. He had a feeling of being not alone. He was glad to grasp the handlebars of his bicycle, as a familiar, reassuring physical fact, and he pedalled back to the police house without completing the last leg of his beat. His wife noticed his shocked state and remarked that he looked as though he had seen a ghost. 'Perhaps I have,' he replied and then proceeded to tell her of his experience.

Some days later PC Williams met an aged parishioner who once worked at Didlington Hall. Without mentioning the earlier happenings he asked the old man the date on which the previous owner of Didlington had died.

'It was on the fourteenth day of November,' came the reply.

The entry in the policeman's notebook for the fateful night read laconically 'Patrolled Didlington. Examined Church.' The entry was dated 14 November, 1956.

Joan Forman, *Haunted East Anglia*, 1985

Callow Pit

There is a traditional tale connected with Southwood, a small village between Yarmouth and Norwich, concerning golden treasure which lies at the bottom of 'Callow Pit'. This is an ancient cavernous pit which lies on the boundary of Southwood and Moulton. At the end of the 19th century a folklorist collected the tale from a local clergyman, who obtained the account from a middle-aged woman, one of the 39 inhabitants of the parish.

The pit was then in a remote part of the village and had long been avoided by people at night for it was reported that a headless horseman frequently rode past that spot. In the past the pit had been used by smugglers for hiding their contraband.

The woman recounted the popular tale of a large quantity of gold locked in an iron chest that lay submerged in the bottom of Callow Pit, for although now dry and thoroughly searched for treasure it was once deep with water.

Once upon time two daring men who firmly believed in the legend determined to search for the chest. Keeping their plans secret they waited patiently until the waters were at their lowest. They placed their ladders across the pit to form a bridge and worked their way to the middle. By means of a strong staff with an iron hook they fished around in the murky water and eventually caught hold of the ring in the lid of the chest. With great effort the chest was raised onto the temporary bridge. It was decided that the best way to carry their find was to put the staff through the ring, thus bearing the weight of the heavy treasure trove on their shoulders.

The narrator continued that, whether dealing with demons or fairies, the popular belief is that silence is essential to success and in this case one of the men was so excited by their tremendous find that he cried out, 'We've got it safe, and Old Nick himself can't get it back from us!'

The pit was instantly enveloped by a dense sulphuric-smelling vapour and a black hand and arm, said to belong to Satan, was thrust up through the water and seized the coveted chest. A desperate struggle ensued between the three, the chest separated from the ring and returned to its original home never to be seen again. The ring remained on the staff and the disappointed men decided to fix the proof of their adventure to the door of Southwood church which is now a ruin. The ring has now been transferred to the door of nearby Limpenhoe church.

Polly Howat, *Tales of Old Norfolk*, 1991

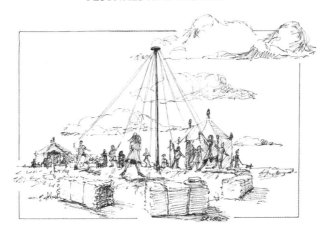

FESTIVALS AND FROLICS

In a farming county like Norfolk, it is natural to find so much writing eager to reflect the colours, flows and rhythms of the seasons, even if the bulk might be tinged with a wistful brush of nostalgia.

The corn harvest, coronation of the year, has been shorn of most of its majesty by mechanisation. Sunday school anniversaries and seaside outings no longer send tingles of excitement through village communities where commuters and computers take precedence over chapel and charabanc.

Even so, harvest suppers, pantomimes and other brands of lively home-made entertainment pay more than lip service to the 'good old days', while a few still stay faithful to the fun and generosity of St Valentine on February 14th.

Although excuses to celebrate Norwich City's soccer fortunes have been in short supply recently, a certain April evening in 1972 calls out for regular replays. And I was there!

Village Valentine

It was Shopman Grey who gave me my first Valentine. Perhaps I should say Shopmen Grey, for there were two brothers in the shop at our village. You could purchase everything from them. They sold clothes, grocery, pieces of pork, oh, and paraffin oil, the odour of which seemed to attach itself to everything.

Their shop was right at the extreme end of our large and straggling village, so one of the brothers brought our grocery round in his horse and cart. He used to come in at the door and begin dumping his wares on the table as he sang out his cheerful greeting – but not to me, I was too young. Then one day he did speak to me:– 'I should thing you are old enough now to have a Valentine, eh, young lady?' he said. I do not think I answered. Granny did however. She said in her sharp voice that she should think so and-all, for she spent quite as much with Shopman Grey as did anyone in the village, and there had never been a Valentine yet.

Smiling, he called me to him, and placed in my hand a stout brown paper bag, the kind we had our chickens maize delivered in. It was twisted over at the top, and weighed a lot. I tried to wait until Granny could come, but they were so long talking over the business of the village, and making up another order for the following week, that my curiosity got the better of me. Untwisting the top of the bag I peeped inside. There in the dim interior I saw two oranges, and a whole lot of other things.

At last Granny came, and together we went through the contents. Besides the oranges, there were several green and sour looking apples, at which Granny grunted, muttering that he might as well have kept them. Next came a screw of paper containing bull's eyes, and another with a variety of sugar coated sweets, the kind one never sees these days.

Last of all there was a small packet of biscuits, and though I have tried many times since to purchase that kind, I have never been able to do so.

All those things of my own! I looked up at Granny, waiting for her pleased look of surprise, but all she said was – 'and so he ought, all the money I spend with him', but I hugged the bag to me. Now I was like all the other children for Shopman Grey had been treating all his customers' children in the same way, it was just because I was little that I had not qualified.

Ida Fenn, Tales of Norfolk, 1976

Sensitive gifts

February 14th, 1871: As an instance of the practical and sensible idea of valentines prevailing in Norfolk, the following were sent to different members of our family this year: to my wife a pair of fine fowls ready for cooking; to myself a book and a leather purse; to my elder daughter two pairs of kid gloves; to one of my sons a meeschaum pipe; to my younger daughter two pairs of kid gloves, a valuable opal ring, a satchell and a box of cambric pocket-handkerchiefs.

Rev. Benjamin Armstrong, A Norfolk Diary, 1871

Patriotic duty

23 April, Saturday: How typical of this place! Today is not only our national day, the feast of Saint George, but also the birthday of our greatest writer, William Shakespeare. Yet here there is almost no sign that they are aware of either festival. There is a limp rag, which may or may not be the flag of St George, hanging from the flagpole of the church, but as far as I can tell the day goes otherwise unrecognised outside this house.

I myself invited the Vicar and Lord Silver-Darling to join me for the occasion, and also allowed Miss Pickerel to come. His Lordship was unable to attend, but sent a most gracious apology.

So we were three that sat down to the 'roast beef of Old England', accompanied, for some reason, by a nasty doughy substance that Maud calls 'domplings', which I am afraid to say the vicar ate with his knife. After dinner I gave a selection of suitable readings, finishing with that stirring speech from Richard II, Act II, Scene i; 'This royal throne of Kings ... this dear, dear land.' As a matter of taste I omitted the line about 'this teeming womb' – I fear the Bard does tend to vulgarity at times.

Miss Pickerel paid rapt attention throughout, while Rev. Mullett closed his eyes and nodded in concentration, with only the occasional murmur escaping his lips. Indeed, he remained thus for some time after I had finished, so moved was he. Eventually we had to shake him to bring him out of his reverie. In conclusion, we sang Mr Blake's 'Jerusalem', which Miss Pickerel accompanied on her violoncello. At least the three of us have done our patriotic duty today.

Chris Sugden and Sid Kipper, Prewd and Prejudice, 1994

Beating the bounds

The ancient custom of 'perambulation,' or 'beating the bounds,' was revived, many years ago, by the late Canon Nock, of Bressingham, and continued annually until his death in 1960.

In the cool of a Rogationtide evening, just before Ascension Day, the Rector, his wardens, Anglican supporters, Free Church people and Salvationists, assembled near the village memorial. After a welcome, and prayers, the procession moved along High Street, to the melodious accompaniment of the Diss Salvation Army Band, halting to sing hymns at the cottages of the aged who could not perambulate.

Blessings were invoked for a bountiful harvest by representatives of the various groups, and so they continued through the village for a final rally about a half-mile 'up the Common' (all traces of the former Common have gone, though many houses 'stand back' on its former boundary).

In keeping with tradition, the participants resorted to the Village Hall for refreshments – the hall being an ancient barn, restored and adapted for community use.

Bressingham is rich in its parish records. The ceremony of perambulation can be traced through nearly four centuries. Even in the reign of Queen Elizabeth I, 'Goeing the Boundes' was a convivial occasion, for the church-wardens recorded paying 'for bere at the perambulation,' and later 'for beere and cakes when we went procession.'

In the 17th century, other luxuries were added, for 'bread, cakes, chese, bere, tobaco and pipes' appeared in the accounts. So, too, did the expense of providing 'wooden crosses,' which were erected at strategic points in the parish boundary, or nailed to prominent trees.

Beating the bounds was no casual country ramble, for ploughed fields, hedges, ditches, ponds and streams all had to be negotiated in this exacting 12-mile test of endurance. Small wonder that they halted at vantage points to rest, offer prayers, consume those provisions and smoke their churchwarden pipes!

Eric Pursehouse, *Waveney Valley Studies*, May 1962

Choir of dahlias

Eggs were chosen with care and sacrifice. Potatoes were scrubbed clean. Parsnips were washed to a creamy yellow and the apples polished until they shone. Marrows and pumpkins were always something of a novelty for they had often been engraved with a text or a line from a hymn in their early days of growth, so that by the time the marrow or pumpkin was ready for cutting the letters stood out clear and bold on their hard skin. By the time we staggered with them to the chapel it was like carrying the Commandment tablets inscribed by Moses himself.

Sheaves of corn were given by farmers. A harvest loaf was baked and presented by one of the town's bakers, and even a sack of coal was given by one of the coalmen. There were exotic gifts like peaches and pomegranates burning like braziers. There were bunches of grapes and baskets of oranges, boxes of nuts, packets of figs and hands of bananas. To walk into chapel on Harvest Sunday was like falling into the hold of a ship just back from the distant tropics. For children not used to seeing such abundance it was like being taken to a pantomime or shown into Aladdin's cave. Flowers hid the pulpit, and often the preacher. We had a choir of dahlias and pillars of chrysanthemums. There was a sweet smell of apples and a tangy whiff of celery. The choir-master always told us that there was a fieldmouse still hiding in one of the sheaves of corn, a tame threat to prevent us from stripping the ears and rubbing them in our hands to find the sweet kernels for eating.

Edward Storey, *The Solitary Landscape*, 1975

Angels to rescue

Today a friend and I discussed the George VI Coronation Procession in Norwich, and afterwards I hunted up some particulars of the old Norwich pageants, which were performed by the City Guilds and were both costly and elaborate displays. There was an account of the 'Creation of the World' when evidently everything did not go 'all right on the night'.

The Creation itself was successfully accomplished, the cocks and hens, cows and sheep being produced in person. Adam then arrived to admire them accompanied by a large mastiff, who guarded him when he lay down to sleep. The Creator appeared to extract his rib preparatory to the manufacture of Eve, but the mastiff objected, nor would he obey the calls and whistles of the angels (equipped with goose feather wings) in the background. At last he was placated and a rib of beef was displayed to the audience, and the Creator turned his back to produce Eve, apparently from Adam's side, but in reality from the trapdoor behind him. In the struggle to get her out he unfortunately trod on the mastiff, who, already sorely tried, promptly sank his teeth into Eve's leg. A general riot ensued, saved by the goose-winged angels, who rushed on the scene and with hearty kicks managed to restore order, consoling the mastiff with Adam's rib, when the play proceeded as before.

Lilias Rider Haggard, *Norfolk Life*, 1943

Harvest horkey

In East Anglia, from very early times, the ingathering of the harvest has been celebrated with divers quaint customs and merry rites; customs and rites summed up in the harvest-frolic, or *Horkey*, a word which has long been a puzzle to etymologists. The Rev. R. Forby, the first writer to seriously record the locutions of Norfolk and Suffolk (in his *Vocabulary of East Anglia*, 2 vols., 1840), says, that the word is intractable to an etymologist, but rather weakly suggests that it may be derived from the hallooing which forms so marked a feature of the horkey. Nall, a very industrious glossarist, compares the work with Norse *hauka*, to shout; Welsh *hwa*, Med. Latin *huccas*, a cry. Hence hawker, huckster. Dr Husenbeth, a learned antiquary, had no doubt that *horkey* was a corruption of *haut cri*, from the loud shouting with which the *horkey* load was brought in. Hoaky is brought home with hollowin, said *Poor Robin* in 1676. The word is variously spelt hawkey, hoaky, hockay, but mostly horkey, and I am of the opinion – suggested long ago in *Notes and Queries* – that it is derived from the hock-cart or hock-load, of which Herrick sings:–

The harvest swains and wenches bound
For joy to see the hock-càrt crown'd'

The hock-cart being the *high*, brimming cart load, crowned with a harvest-maiden, a kern-baby, or a green bough, on its triumphal progress from the field to the homestead.

Home came the jovial Horkey load,
Last of the whole year's crop;
And Grace amongst the green boughs rode
Right plump upon the top.

James Hooper, 'Horkeys, or harvest frolics' in *Bygone Norfolk*, 1898

Christmas feast

In winter-time, when snow was on the ground, fierce gales blew and fishermen had all made up, the choir was at its best, in fettle as well as in numbers; for did not the great social event of the whole year, the 'Singers' Feast', take place a short time after Christmas!

On Christmas Eve the 'singers', as the choir was always called, went round to all the principal houses to sing carols, when, besides being overwhelmed with hospitality, they would collect subscriptions towards the Singers' Feast.

The feast was held in the old school-room, a long, low, narrow building with brick floor, few windows, and only one small ventilation hole through the thatched roof.

As each singer was allowed to bring one or two guests, the choir at Christmas-time swelled to huge proportions, so that finally almost the whole village would either be at the feast itself, or at least turn up in Sunday best immediately after dinner to join in the games, songs, dancing and general merrymaking.

Old 'Long Tom' Brown, a cavernous giant of some six feet six, had nothing whatever to do with singing, either in church or out, but as he could eat his length in sausages any day, his presence at the feast went without saying, and we boys would struggle for near-by seats in order to get a good view of the prowess of such a redoubtable champion.

The menu was of simple gradeur: first, delicious Norfolk dumplings and beef gravy; then mountains of prime roast beef and boiled mutton, backed up by potatoes, turnips, carrots, and horse-radish and washed down with good six-ale; while the 'sweets' course was represented solely by plum-puddings – lashins of 'em – and brandy sauce; to all of which cheese, celery, and good pickled onions put a fitting coping-stone.

What a row of healthy, happy faces beamed on either side of that long, narrow table; never again, alas, shall I see the like. Old folks, middle-aged couples, blue guernseyed young fishermen with their pretty sweet-hearts, giggling girls and boys.

Oliver Ready, *East Anglian Reminiscences*, 1910

The Harvest Moan

We plough the fields and scatter the good seed on the land,
But after that things never go in quite the way we planned;
The moles and mice and magpies come down to eat the grain;
Before a week is over we must scatter the seed again.

Chorus
All good things around us belong to someone else;
With one accord we thank the Lord and tighten up our belts.

This time some seeds are left to sprout and poke their young heads out;
They seem both hale and hearty, until we have a drought.
So with the sweat from off our brows we irrigate the crop,
Until at last the rain begins – and then it just won't stop.

But when the downpour ceases a few young plants remain;
The sun lifts up their heads and we begin to hope again.
To think that such fine healthy plants grew from such tiny seeds!
But on examination we find most of them are weeds.

What's left when we have weeded begins to turn to brown,
The time has come to harvest all that has not been blown down.
The yield is poor – in fact, there is just sufficient there
To plough the fields and scatter on the land again next year.

Chris Sugden and Sid Kipper, *The Ballad of Sid Kipper*, 1996

Acting out

Margaret Paston to John Paston, 24th December, 1459:
Please you to know that I sent your eldest son to my Lady Morley to have knowledge what sports were used in her house at Christmas next following after the decease of my lord, her

husband, And she said that there were no disguisings (acting), nor harping, luting or singing, nor any lewd sports, but just playing at the tables (backgammon) and chess and cards. Such sports she gave her folk leave to play and no other. Your son did his errand right well, as you will hear later. I sent your younger son to Lady Stapleton's and she said the same as Lady Morley, that this had been the practice in places of worship (honourable households) where she had been...

Paston Letters

Centenary show

I shall long remember that centenary Royal Norfolk Show at Keswick. It seemed to be the quintessence of all the agricultural shows I have ever seen and enjoyed. It had a perfect setting with the tiny round-towered church and its surrounding trees for the background, and the grey hall, like an unobtrusive host, offering the hospitality of its lawn to the august gathering of vice-presidents, yet modestly concealing itself behind the grand stand. The weather also was perfect, at any rate for show purposes. For some reason my memory retains the traces only of sunshine at these shows, and conveniently excludes the melancholy of dripping tents, wet feet, mired ways and umbrellas round the ring, on other occasions. It was perhaps best forgotten for the time being, that this particular sunshine was also the continuation of a drought that will make 1947 a black year in farming history – following, as it does, the worst winter of frost and flood in living memory. I believe even farmers forgot it for a little while – enjoying while they could the success of their show. In its greenness and its air of carefree prosperity the whole thing did not seem quite real. It contained so much of the old England mixed up with the new. It did not look as if there had been a world war, and before that an agricultural depression, and before that another world war, and before that another agricultural depression. It did not look as though the present was lean and hungry, the future anxious and the harvest likely to be scanty. On reflection, it seems to me to have been an illusion brought about by a green park, some hundreds of fine animals, a skilful organisation, and countrymen's determination to make the best of a holiday. On that day it was enough to be contented, like the sleek cattle, and take no thought for the morrow.

Jonathan Mardle, The Best of Jonathan Mardle, 1982

Promotion party

April 24, 1972. And so in the end it all boiled down to Leyton Orient and Brisbane Road, London, E.10. Thousands made the journey, Keith Skipper and I travelling in a photographer colleague's car. It was a scene I shall never forget. Yellow and green adorned vehicles swarmed towards London – reminding me that Saunders had once contemplated trying to change City's first choice colours into an all-red strip – while at Brisbane Road the Orient's red and white favours were brushed aside by a tide of East Anglian enthusiasm.

In the end, and thanks to goals from Foggo and Paddon, a penalty, City won 2–1 and at last banished all the doubts and worries, pessimism and scorn. Loved or unloved, glamorous or not, City were in Division One and Ron Saunders stood at the front of the Brisbane Road stand to accept the plaudits of the crowd. City fans swarmed over the barriers and across the pitch; the players clung to each other in mutually shared joy; champagne appeared in the directors' box; 'On the ball, City,' welled around the ground; the fans sang 'For he's a jolly good fellow,' and a tide of emotion such as the Canaries had not seen since 1958/59 surged and lapped the ground. Later, the City dressing room was besieged by Press pundits and television presenters and cameras, and trainer George Lee was picked up by the players and flung bodily into the bath. Outside in the streets of E.10 the celebrating went on, and it was hours before the straggling column of fans began to think about making its way home. Once all the interviewing and telephoning was done Keith and I slipped away from Brisbane Road, drove a short way home and then stopped for a pint.

The pub was full of City fans. Every pub, it seemed, was full of City fans. Anyway, we were recognised and soon drawn into the party, in the middle of which another shining faced City fan arrived only to dump a big clod of earth on the bar. He was triumphant. 'It's the penalty spot,' he said. I have often wondered what happened to that famous lump of grass.

Bruce Robinson, *Passing Seasons*, 1997

Annual outing

Hanworth 1920:
Our old Rector, 'Uncle', as we called him affectionately, was born a hundred and twenty years ago. He died at eighty, having served our village for forty years.

Every summer there was a booking which Tammy the cabman never forgot. This was to take dear old Uncle to the station for the annual outing to Yarmouth. It was a real village outing financed by Uncle, and one which he enjoyed as much as anybody. Practically everybody was eligible in some way. The men's club, the choir (the same thing as a rule), all the school children and toddlers, and the Mothers Meeting Members.

This was a gathering which met periodically to drink tea, sew and be read to. My mother often did the reading. When asked how she chose suitable books, I remember her saying in her very practical way, 'Oh, those which have a little love and religion in them.'

The children began to congregate in the Grove, hours before they were due to start. For many of the little ones it might be the first ride in the train, but for all it was a red letter day. The children were taken to the station in farm waggons, and when these turned into the Grove they always cheered and shouted. Loading processes took some time, small children were lifted in and told where to sit, and given injunctions about leaning over the side. Boys clambered up the wheels, and those who had been hanging about in the hope of riding one of the horses were pushed up and told to mind what they were about.

When everything had been settled to the satisfaction of the schoolmistress and the men in charge of the waggons, the procession started, waggons first, with one or two bicycles as sort of out riders. There was a good selection of prams and pushcarts following full of toddlers and a few babies with mums anxious to make a day of it too. Lastly with great dignity came Tammy with Uncle and the headmistress in the cab, the Junior having been loaded into the waggon to keep an eye on the children. At the station Uncle had a sixpence ready for every child to spend, and he also provided a slap up tea for the whole party. A generous, lonely old man he loved taking out his flock which was to him his family.

Norfolk Federation of Women's Institutes, *Within Living Memory*, 1972

Whitsun Sports

Summer was heralded by the annual Whitsun sports, a most important day in the annual calendar. For weeks before the event prizes were displayed in the window of Back's shop. Barometers and clocks for the men. Books, shutknives and toys for the children. Money prizes were not given till 1946 as in the early days serious amateur runners from all over North Norfolk competed. The village band, long since defunct, played at the pre-war games, and a crowd of over a thousand would be expected. After the war the revived games featured decorated carts, bicycles and fancy dress for children.

Family reunions took place around the perimeter of the track as families from the surrounding villages came in their traps and carts. Children jumped up and off the tumbrils placed as grandstands with bales of hay on which to sit. Picnics were opened and friends joined in the revels. If ever there was a 'throwback' to the old Maytime revels it was the Whitsun Sports.

Today's sports are a pale shadow of the old days, but all credit goes to those who have revived the tradition in the face of bus and car excursions. After the Whitsun sports came the 'treats' from church and chapel already mentioned. Then the cricket season began. Cricket in Hindringham was almost a religion. The same faces appeared each year and competition with other villages was keen indeed. No cricket team was complete without one or more of the Howard family and during the thirties and after the war Ethel Howard, popularly known as 'Tink', was an ever faithful scorer.

Sheila Wyer, *Requiem For A Village*, 1983

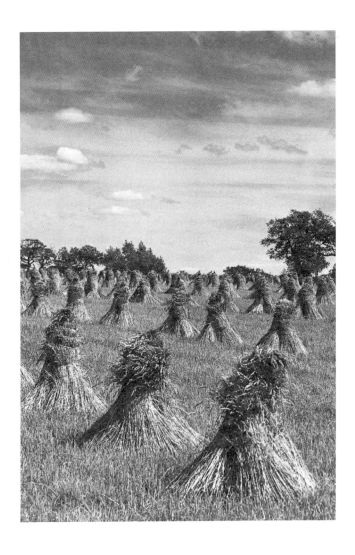

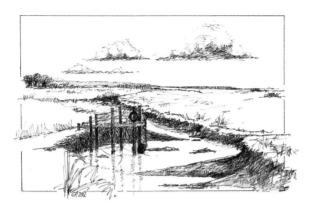

UNFADING CHARMS

This was at once the easiest and yet most difficult section to compile. Easiest because even its harshest critics agree Norfolk holds fast to special qualities, geography bequeathing an isolation to shape character and largely protect it. Most difficult because so many genuine tributes deserve inclusion.

I have had to satisfy myself with just a few plums, shared between illustrious visitors like William Cobbett and H.V. Morton and those soaked in Norfolk ways such as Lilias Rider Haggard and Ted Ellis. They head a lengthy cavalcade stretching back over the centuries.

One of my favourite poems, Autumn Evening in a Norfolk Lane, provides a perfect ending to this volume. It was written by Leslie Jolly in a prisoner-of-war camp in Java in 1942. Some of his poems were buried by Australian friends after being wrapped in tin foil from tea chests.

At the end of the war, the author found most of those poems and the foil had been eaten by white ants. However, he kept these verses with him. They survived the Japanese search, unfading pictures of a homeland to which he was so grateful to return.

Slow but sure

A first visit to Norfolk is, I venture to say, a surprise. This county unfolds itself bit by bit as one of the least spoiled districts in England. Its people, its architecture, its customs, its scenery are distinct and individual. It is still geographically an island. It is separated from Suffolk by the Rivers Waveney and Little Ouse and from Cambridgeshire by the Ouse and the Nene. Its eastbound boundary is the North Sea, which beats itself along the ninety miles of the Norfolk coastline. This peculiarity is, no doubt, in some measure responsible for the individuality of Norfolk. You feel when in Norfolk that you are in a country, not a county.

*   *   *   *   *

I entered a land of broad, gold cornfields, silvery acres of oats and barley. The church towers were round and made of smooth chipped flint, so that they looked like a mosaic of blue-grey glass. The people I met were remarkable for their physique and their speech, a strange, slow burr. When I asked them a question they paused a while before replying, unlike the West-countryman, who answers immediately, or the Cornishman, who is ready with an answer before you have stopped speaking. The Norfolk people take their time. They are slow but sure – until they make up their minds about you.

H.V. Morton, *The Land of the Vikings*, 1928

Market day

AYLSHAM, NORFOLK: The livestock market held just outside the centre of this beautiful Georgian town every Monday morning is one of the great rituals of mid-Norfolk. Anyone living or even visiting the county should see it at least once; though go early - the place rapidly becomes crowded. Many of the rural communities surrounding you are of a vintage Thomas Hardy would have recognised and cherished, and some faces have the rich, comfortable character and idiosyncratic lines of an old oak settle. Yet don't be deceived by the rustic appearance: the leather patches on elbows, the subdued tones of the check, the tear, perhaps, at the jacket's shoulder, the unfashionable cut of lapel or trousers. Beneath that arched eyebrow is a shrewd instrument for judging life and its affairs. A fascinating portion of the market is the sale of household goods. Long before the auctioneer and his excited throng have moved systematically down the rows of lots, the prospective purchasers have examined and valued them. One of these lots can consist of an extraordinary mix: a disembodied lawn mower, a second-hand chainsaw, coils of barbed wire, a box of yellowed 1950s paperbacks and a beautiful easy-chair that might go for scores of pounds down the King's Road. Here, in the heated moments of the bidding, its price might leap upwards in units of fifty pence and end after six forefingers have been raised momentarily. If Aylsham market is an expression of an older England, the cafe, standing in the middle of the grounds, suggests a forgotten age. At this time of the year the place is always busy, the windows steamed over and the interior thick with tobacco smoke. The bread is always white, the cakes home-made and the tea strong, hot and at a price that would give any Little Chef manager a bout of palpitations.

Mark Cocker, 'A Country Diary' in *The Guardian*, 11 November 1991

Childhood echoes

I went over to the other side of Norwich to fetch some pullets. The birch woods lit by a brilliant sun were all gleaming silver, their bushy, fine-twigged tops flushed with the purple bloom which comes to many trees at the first stirring of the sap. The plough lands were dried to a warm russet, and on the light soils pale tan, except where the labouring plough teams left broad dark bars in their wake. I arrived at one of those Norfolk farms which seem still quite untouched by the coming of machinery, as farms were in one's childhood. The duck pond and the comfortable huddle of buildings crowded together under the shadow of a big barn. A placid sow outstretched in the sunshine contentedly suckled her numerous progeny, next door to a couple of horses busy at a midday feed. In the background two smiling women were perched on stools trimming black currant cuttings with skilled fingers, and tying them in bundles to soak in the pond before setting. The house itself gave the impression that it had been there since the beginning; that successive generations had altered its outward seeming to their several tastes – leaving its bones untouched, so that the date 1830 sat unconvincingly upon a re-faced Tudor porch. There may have been cars and tractors and electricity and silos in the background, but I did not see them. I collected my pullets, a nice lot of North Holland Blues, supposed to be the last word in utility breeds, but owing not a little (to judge from their appearance) to our old friend the Plymouth Rock, unless I am much mistaken.

Lilias Rider Haggard, *Norfolk Notebook*, 1946

Song of praise

NORFOLK, although no mountain ranges
  Girdle you plains with a bastioned height,
Yet is your landscape rich in changes,
  Filling the eye with delight –
Heath-clad uplands and lonely dingles,
  Slow streams stealing through level meads.
Flats where the marsh with the ocean mingles,
  Meres close guarded by sentinel reeds.

Never a mile but some church-tower hoary
  Stands for a witness, massive and tall,
How men furthered God's greater glory –
  Blakeney and Cley and Salle.
Never a village but in its borders
  Signs of a stormy past remain,
Walls that were manned by Saxon warders,
  Barrows that guard the bones of the Dane.

Deep in your heart Rome left her traces,
  Normans held your manors in fee,
Italy lent you her southern graces,
  Dutchman bridled your sea.
Flemings wove you their silks and woollens,
  Romany magic still to you clings,
And the fairest daughter of all the Bullens
  Blent your blood with that of your Kings.

Yours are the truest names in England –
  Overy Staithe and Icknield Way,
Waveney river, Ringmere and Ringland,
  Wymondham and Wormegay.
Land of windmills and brown-winged wherries,
  Gliding along with the gait of Queens;
Land of the Broads, the dykes, and the ferries,
  Land of the sounds, the brecks, the denes.

Gipsy lore, the heart of his stories,
  Borrow gleaned in his Norwich home.
Broadland, aflame with sunset glories,
  Fired the vision of Crome.
Tombland's echo throughout the pages
  Of Browne like a stately Requiem runs;
Nelson, 'a name to resound for ages,'
  Crowns the roll of your hero sons.

Charles L. Graves, *East Anglian Verse*,
E. A. Goodwyn and J. C. Baxter (eds), 1974

Black diamonds

If it was startling to leave behind so soon the Essex fields, where the young corn was vivid with sap in the blade, it was perhaps even more startling to see the thatch-and-plaster give way to flint. Norfolk is the very matrix of flint, and we at home, with our cobble paths and cobble sheds, have no idea how lovely the knapped flint can look when built into a wall that seems to hold the hot earth's core in its shining depths.

To build with flint is seemingly to build for ever: these brilliant, black-hearted cottages of Breckland appear as new and neat to-day as when they were erected. In the spring sunshine they glinted as if black diamonds had been cemented into the regular courses; but they can look equally lovely in rain, themselves bright as rain-drops. Next to pargeted plaster, which familiarity and prejudice, if not affection, would have me prefer, I can think of no more characterful building material, though I admit it is not to everybody's taste and needs time, perhaps, to appreciate.

C. Henry Warren, *The Scythe in the Apple Tree*, 1953

Excellent farmers

Monday, 24 Dec:
Went from Bergh Apton to Norwich in the morning, and from Norwich to London during the day, carrying with me great admiration of and respect for this county of *excellent farmers*, and hearty, open and spirited men. The Norfolk people are quick and smart in their motions and in their speaking. Very neat and *trim* in all their farming concerns, and very skilful. Their land is good, their roads are level, and the bottom of their soil is dry, to be sure; and these are great advantages; but they are diligent, and make the most of everything. Their management of all sorts of stock is most judicious; they are careful about manure; their teams move quickly; and, in short, it is a county of most excellent cultivators. The churches in Norfolk are generally large and the towers lofty. They have all been well built at first. Many of them are of the Saxon architecture. They are, almost all (I do not remember an exception), placed on the *highest* spots to be found near where they stand; and, it is curious enough, that the contrary practice should have prevailed in *hilly* countries, where they are generally found in valleys and in low, sheltered dells, even in those valleys! These churches prove that the people of Norfolk and Suffolk were always a superior people in point of wealth, while the size of them proves that the country parts were, at

one time, a great deal more populous then they now are. The great drawbacks on the beauty of these counties are, their flatness and their want of fine woods; but to those who can dispense with these, Norfolk, under a wise and just government, can have nothing to ask more than Providence and the industry of man have given.

William Cobbett, *Rural Rides*, 1821

Last furrow

The sun disappeared in the west, small and smoky. The air grew colder. Frost in the shade by the lower hedge began to look whiter. The engine seemed to be noisier. I began to feel that farming wasn't so interesting after all, and how much nicer to be writing beside a fire. One more round, I thought, before leaving the tractor by the hedge, water drained and cloth tied over it. The flights of starlings had gone across the sky; the gulls had left, too. Well, it was the last round, and now the mind must stop thinking, lest it get pessimistic. Go home, wash, change, and relax. Coming to the top again, I ran round 'empty' along the headland – which had been plowed in the summer, and was now a pleasing brown of half-rotted turf and broken tree-root – and set in along the last furrow. In front of me was a whiteness, where a long snake of turf had curled back; and stopping the tractor, I got off and went stiffly forward, to stand above a pair of delicate grey wings spread motionless on the frosting grass. One of the black-headed gulls, alighting and dipping for a worm, had been caught by the back-curling furrow. It must be suffocated, I thought, as I knelt to heave back the turf. It was heavy, and I felt tired, but at last I got it free, expecting the bird to be limp and crushed; but with a turn of its head and a feeble scream from its red mouth, it elbowed itself lightly into the air, and flew slowly away.

Henry Williamson, *Green Fields and Pavements*, 1943

Here, at the Tide's Turning

You close your eyes and see

                the stillness of
the mullet-nibbled arteries, samphire
on the mudflats almost underwater,
and on the saltmarsh whiskers of couch-grass
twitching, waders roosting, sea-lavender
faded to ashes.

          In the dark or almost dark
shapes sit on the staithe muttering of plickplack,
and greenshanks, and zos birds:

                a duck arrives
in a flap, late for a small pond party.

The small yard's creak and groan and lazy rap,
muffled water music.

          One sky-streamer,
pale and half-frayed, still dreaming of colour.

Water and earth and air quite integral:
all Waterslain one sombre aquarelle.

From the beginning, and last year, this year,
you can think of no year when you have
not sat on this stub of a salt-eaten stanchion.

Dumbfounded by such tracts of marsh and sky –
the void swirled round you and pressed against you –
you've found a mercy in small stones.

This year, next year, you cannot think
of not returning: not to perch in the blue
hour on this blunt jetty, not to wait, as of right,
for the iron hour and the turning of the tide.

You cross the shillying and the shallows
and, stepping on to the marsh, enter
a wilderness.

Quick wind works around you.

You are engulfed in a wave of blue flames.

No line that is not clear cut and severe,
nothing baroque or bogus. The voices
of young children rehearsing on the staithe
are lifted from another time.

This is
battleground. Dark tide fills the winking pulks,
floods the mud-canyons.

This flux, this anchorage.

Here you watch, you write, you tell the tides.

You walk clean into the possible.

Kevin Crossley Holland, *Selected Poems*, 2001

Pastoral peace

Surlingham,
April 22nd, 1964

'And this our life, exempt from public haunt,
  Finds tongues in trees, books in the running brooks,
Sermons in stones and good in everything.'
  'I would not change it.'

So Shakespeare in 'As You Like It' forestalled Gilbert White in presenting the gentle outlook of the country philosopher living close to nature. Now, 400 years after the poet's birth, the English countryside is vastly changed, yet in this thickly populated island miraculously there are still wildernesses 'exempt from public haunt'; where 'daisies pied and violets blue, and lady-smocks all silver-white, and cuckoo-buds of yellow hue do paint the meadows with delight,' and great green spaces where 'the lark at heaven's gate sings.'

Here in East Anglia we have largely escaped the stranglehold of industrial expansion and the sprawling over-growth of cities. But we have been reminded recently of what professional planners have in mind for the future; a more even distribution of industry, homes and people over the length and breadth of the land until ultimately it will become impossible to find a secluded wilderness.

No place will be 'exempt from public haunt'. With this threat in the offing I make no apology for standing out against it for what I believe to be the ultimate good.

I am very jealous for the pastoral peace of the East Anglian countryside. If it is destroyed, where will town-dwellers and all the sick-of-suburbs people turn to find unspoiled country? Let us remain a breathing space for the cure of souls rejoicing in honest agriculture, forestry and the like and cherishing the serene beauty of our Broads and coast. I am sure we can still do this and live.

Ted Ellis, *Eastern Daily Press*, 22 April 1964

Autumn Evening in a Norfolk Lane

The nodding mare strains slowly down the lane.
  'Neath guardian oaks, age-old, that gloom all day
High mossy banks, where hazel bushes hide
  Rich store for squirrels. The footfalls die away.
The brambled gateway shows the stubble bare
  Of barley sheaves. A lone cloud veils the moon,
As if to mourn the scarlet poppies fled
          That flamed at noon.
Within the deep recesses of a wood
  A shot dispels the silence; pigeons wing
Their urgent way, and inwardly I see
  A leafy glade, a piteous fluttering
Of blood and feathers, never more to dream
  And coo its music on the topmost bough
Or silhouetted on the hill, descry
          The lonely plough.

The distant echoes fade and stillness blends
  Its healing virtue with the gathering shade.
Unseen, a field mouse scampers stealthy by;
  Unheard, a stoat pursues his nightly raid.
The evening haze is heavy with the scent
  Of wind-blown apples and the pungent tang
Of many scutch-fires that, primeval, on
          The night airs hang.

As far off chimes recall my lagging feet.
  A frail bent woman on an old man's arm
Looms in the dusk and tremulous returns
  A faint 'Goodnight'. Their autumn free from harm
Of stoat or fowler, a harvest only shows
  Of summer heats of toil. They trusting keep
Their faith, and quietly, like children tires.
          They wait on sleep.

L. H. Jolly (Glodock Prison, 1942) *East Anglian Verse*,
E. A. Goodwyn and J. C. Baxter (eds), 1974

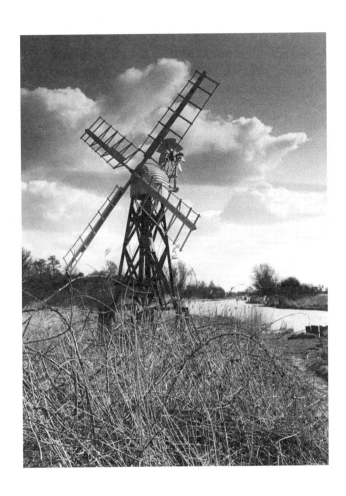

ACKNOWLEDGEMENTS

Every effort has been made to secure permission; nonetheless, we may have failed to trace the copyright holder. We apologise for any apparent negligence.

The editor and publishers gratefully acknowledge the following for permission to reprint copyright material in this book:

Rachel Anderson, for permission to reprint the extract from *The Poacher's Son*.

Robert Bagshaw, for permission to reprint extract from *Norfolk Remembered*.

Jim Baldwin Publishing, for permission to reprint the extract from Ted Eales' *Countryman's Memoirs*.

Dr. Anthony Batty Shaw, for permission to reprint extract from *Norfolk and Norwich Medicine*.

John Baxter, for permission to reprint extracts and poems from: *East Anglian Reminiscences*; and *East Anglian Verse*.

Mrs N. H. A. Cheyne, for permission to reprint extracts from Lilias Rider Haggard's: *I Walked by Night*; *The Rabbit Skin Cap*; *Norfolk Life*; *Norfolk Notebook*; and *A Country Scrapbook*.

Countryside Books, for permission to reprint extracts from: Norfolk Federation of Women's Institutes' *Within Living Memory: a collection of Norfolk reminiscences*; and Polly Howat's *Tales of Old Norfolk*.

Kevin Crossley Holland and Rogers, Coleridge & White Ltd, for permission to reprint 'Here at the Tide's Turning' © Kevin Crossley Holland.

Dovecote Press, for permission to reprint the extract from R. O'Brien's *East Anglian Curiosities*.

Mrs Phyllis Ellis, for permission to reprint the extract from Ted Ellis' *Countryside Recollections*.

Faber and Faber Ltd., for permission to reprint the extract from R. Ketton-Cremer's *Norfolk Portraits*.

Mrs Joan Forman, for permission to reprint the extract from *Haunted East Anglia*.

The Guardian, for permission to reprint Mark Cocker's 'Country Diary' which appeared in *The Guardian*, 11 November 1991.

HarperCollins, for permission to reprint the extract from Brian Aldiss's *Remembrance Day*.

Gabrielle Hatfield, for permission to reprint the extract from her *Country Remedies*.

Professor John Hibbs, for permission to reprint the extract from his *The Country Chapel*.

Thomas Hinde, for permission to reprint the extract from *A Field Guide to the English Country Parson*.

Hodder and Stoughton Ltd., for permission to reprint extracts from Peter Bagshaw's *The Gap in the Dunes*.

Mrs Jean Joice, for permission to reprint the extract from Dick Joice's, *Full Circle*.

Mrs. Hilda Jolly, for permission to reprint extracts from Cyril Jolly's:
History of the East Dereham Methodist Circuit; Henry Blogg of Cromer; and
The Spreading Flame.

John Kett, for permission to reprint poems from: *Remembered in Rhyme*;
Tha's a Rum'un Bor!; Tha's a Rum'un Tew!; and *A Late Lark Singing.*

Les King, for permission to reprint extracts from *King of Sport.*

Larks Press for permission to reprint extracts from David Armstrong's
A Short History of Norfolk Cricket; and Susan Yaxley's *The Rector Will Be
Glad – A Norfolk Parish Miscellany 1898–1920.*

Merlin Press, for permission to reprint the extract from Roy Groves'
Sharpen the Sickle! A History of the Farm-workers' Union.

pHIL nICHOLLS, for permission to reprint his poem from *The Dreams of
Grandfather Heron.*

Nostalgia Publications, for permission to reprint the extract from Philip
Yaxley's, *Looking Back at Norfolk Cricket.*

Peake Associates, for permission to reprint the extract from Jennifer
Westwood's *Gothick Norfolk.*

Phillimore & Co. Ltd., for permission to reprint the extract from
P. Richards' *King's Lynn.*

Tom Pocock, for permission to reprint the extract from his *Norfolk – Pimlico
County History Guides.*

Laurence Pollinger Ltd., and the Estate of C. H. Warren for permission to
reprint the extract from C. H. Warren's *The Scythe in the Apple Tree.*

Poppyland Publishing, for permission to reprint extracts from P. Brooks'
Weybourne; and from *Crabs and Shannocks.*

The Random House Group, for permission to reprint the extract from
Arnold Wesker's *As Much As I Dare.*

Malcolm Rix, for permission to reprint the extract from *Never Forget.*

Bruce Robinson, for permission to reprint extracts from his *Passing Seasons.*

Routledge and Kegan Paul, for permission to reprint extracts from
W. H. Barrett and R. P. Garrod's , *East Anglian Folklore*; and
A. Randell's *Fenland Memories.*

Maurice de Soissons, for permission to reprint the extract from *Brancaster
Staithe – the Story of a Norfolk Fishing Village.*

Abner Stein Literary Agency, for permission to reprint the extract from
M. Jefferies' *Shadows in the Watchgate.*

Edward Storey, for permission to reprint extracts from *North Bank Night*;
A Man in Winter; and *The Solitary Landscape.*

Richard Tilbrook, for permission to reprint the extract from Rosemary
Tilbrook's *A Year in the Countryside.*

Lavinia Trevor Literary Agency, for permission to reprint the extract from
Tim Wilson's *Heartsease.*

A. P. Watt Ltd. on behalf of Rosemary Beresford, B. W. Beresford, Ruth
Longman and J. C. Beresford, for permission to reprint extracts from
James Woodforde's *The Diary of a Country Parson: 1758–1802.*

The Henry Williamson Literary Estate, for permission to reprint extracts
from Henry Williamson's *The Story of a Norfolk Farm*; and *Green Fields
and Pavements.*

REFERENCES

Aldiss, B., *Remembrance Day*, HarperCollins, 1992

Amis, A., *From Dawn to Dusk*, self-published, 1992

Anderson, R., *The Poacher's Son*, Oxford University Press, 1982

Andrews, W. (ed.), *Bygone Norfolk*, William Andrews and Co., 1898

Armstrong, B., *A Norfolk Diary*, George Harrap, 1949

Armstrong, D., *A Short History of Norfolk Cricket*, Larks Press, 1990

Bagshaw, P., *The Gap in the Dunes*, Hodder and Stoughton, 1959

Bagshaw, R., *Norfolk Remembered*, Geo. R. Reeve, 1989

Barker, G., 'On a Friend's Escape from Drowning off the Norfolk Coast' in *Norfolk (Poet's England series)*, Brentham Press, 1994

Barrett, W. H. and Garrod, R. P., *East Anglian Folklore*, Routledge and Kegan Paul, 1976

Batty Shaw, A., *Norfolk and Norwich Medicine*, The Norwich Medico-Chirurgical Society, 1992

Bell, T., *On the Ball, City*, Wensum Books, 1972

Berlyn, A., *Sunrise-Land*, Jarrold and Sons, 1894

Berry, P., *Earth Musk and Country Dark*, Starling Press, 1985

Blyth, J., *Juicy Joe*, William Brendon, 1903

Blyth, J., *Longshore Lass*, F. V. White, 1910

Brandon-Cox, *Mud on my Boots*, East Countryman, 1994

Brooks, P., *Weybourne*, Poppyland Publishing, 1984

Carter, M. J., *Peasants and Poachers*, The Boydell Press, 1980

Chestney, B., *Island of Terns*, Quiller Press, 1993

Cobbett, W., *Rural Rides*, first published 1821

Cocker, M., 'A Country Diary' in *The Guardian*, 11 November, 1991

Crossley Holland, K., 'Here at the Tide's Turning' in *Selected Poems*, Enitharmon Press, 2001

Crowley, J., and Reid, A., (eds), *The Poor Law in Norfolk 1700-1850*, EARO, 1983

Davies, H., 'The Hovelleers' in *Crabs and Shannocks* (edited by K. Lee, P. Stibbons and M. Warren), Poppyland Publishing, 1983

Dew, W. N., *A Dyshe of Norfolk Dumplings*, 1898, reprinted EP Publishing, 1973

Dickens, C., *David Copperfield*, first published 1850

Douglas Brown, R., *East Anglia 1942*, Terence Dalton, 1988

Eales, T., *Countryman's Memoirs*, Jim Baldwin Publishing, 1986

Edwards, G., *From Crow-scaring to Westminster*, Labour Publishing Company, 1922

Ellis, T., *Countryside Recollections*, Wilson-Poole Publishers, 1982

Etheridge, F., *Salt on a White Plate*, self-published, 1989

Fenn, I., *Tales of Norfolk*, Geo. R. Reeves, 1976

Forman, J., *Haunted East Anglia*, Jarrold Publishing, 1985

Glyde, J. Jnr., *Folklore and Customs of Norfolk*, 1872, reprinted EP Publishing, 1973

Goodwyn, E. A., and Baxter, J. C. (eds), *East Anglian Reminiscences*, The Boydell Press, 1973

Goodwyn, E. A., and Baxter, J. C. (eds), *East Anglian Verse*, The Boydell Press, 1974

Grapes, S., *The Boy John Letters*, Norfolk News Co., 1958

Groves, R., *Sharpen the Sickle! A history of the farm-workers' union*, Merlin Press, 1981

Hales, J., *The East Wind*, Charles Veal, 1969

Hales, J. and Bennett, W., *Looking at Norfolk*, Geo. R. Reeve, 1971

Harland, E., *No Halt at Sunset*, The Boydell Press, 1951

Hatfield, G., *Country Remedies*, The Boydell Press, 1994

Hibbs, J., *The Country Chapel*, David and Charles, 1988

Hinde, T., *A Field Guide to the English Country Parson*, Heinemann, 1983

Holbrook, D., *Getting It Wrong with Uncle Tom*, Mousehold Press, 1998

Hooper, J., 'Horkeys, or harvest frolics' in *Bygone Norfolk* (edited by W. Andrews), 1898

Howat, P., *Tales of Old Norfolk*, Countryside Books, 1991

Hudson, W. H., *Afoot in England*, Hutchinson, 1909

Hudson, W. H., *Adventures among Birds*, J. M. Dent, 1923

Jefferies, M., *Shadows in the Watchgate*, Grafton, 1991

Jeffery, P., *East Anglian Ghosts, Legends and Lore*, Old Orchard Press, 1988

Jessopp, A., *Arcady: For Better For Worse*, Fisher Unwin, 1887

Jessup, G., *East Anglian Magazine*, 1957

Joice, D., *Full Circle*, The Boydell Press, 1991

Jolly, C., *History of the East Dereham Methodist Circuit*, Geo R. Reeve, 1955

Jolly, C., *Henry Bloggs of Cromer*, Jim Baldwin, 1958

Jolly, C., *The Spreading Flame*, Jim Baldwin, 1974

Kett, J., *Remembered in Rhyme*, Baron Publishing, 1957

Kett, J., *Tha's a Rum'un Bor!*, Baron Publishing, 1973

Kett, J., *Tha's a Rum'un Tew!*, Baron Publishing, 1975

Kett, J., *A Late Lark Singing*, Minerva Press, 1997

Ketton-Cremer, R. W., *Norfolk Portraits*, Faber and Faber, 1944

King, L., *King of Sport*, Geo. R. Reeves, 1992

Knyvet Wilson, B., *Norfolk Tales and Memories*, Jarrold and Sons, 1930

Knyvet Wilson, B., *More Norfolk Tales and Memories*, Jarrold and Sons, 1931

Lee, K., Stibbons, P., and Warren, M., *Crabs and Shannocks*, Poppyland Publishing, 1983

Mann, M., *The Fields of Dulditch*, 1902, reprinted The Boydell Press, 1976

Mardle, J., *The Best of Jonathan Mardle*, volume one, Albion Books, 1982

Marlowe, C., *People and Places in Marshland*, Burleigh Press, 1927

Marsh, J., *Back to the Land*, Quartet Books, 1982

Morton, H. V., *In Search of England*, Methuen, 1927

Morton, H. V., *The Land of the Vikings*, The Chaucer Press, 1928

nICHOLLS, p., *The Dreams of Grandfather Heron*, Magpie Productions, 1999

Norfolk Federation of Women's Institutes, *Within Living Memory: a collection of Norfolk reminiscences*, Countryside Books, 1972

Norfolk Federation of Women's Institutes, *Within Living Memory: a collection of Norfolk reminiscences*, Countryside Books, 1995

O'Brien, R., *East Anglian Curiosities*, Dovecote Press, 1992

O'Connor, J., *Memories of a Market Trader*, Minimax Books, 1984

Paston Family, *The Illustrated Letters of the Paston Family*, edited by R. Virgoe, Macmillan, 1989

Pestell, R. E., 'Smuggling in Norfolk' in *Norfolk Fair*, 1967

Pestell, R. E., 'Norfolk Eccentrics' in *Norfolk Fair*, 1968

Piggott, E., in *East Anglian Reminiscences*, edited by Goodwyn, E. A., and Baxter, J. C., The Boydell Press, 1974

Pocock, T.. *Norfolk - Pimlico County History Guides*, Pimlico, 1995

Pursehouse, E., *Waveney Valley Studies*, Diss Publishing, 1962

Randell, A., *Sixty Years a Fenman*, Routledge and Kegan Paul, 1966

Randell, A., *Fenland Memories*, Routledge and Kegan Paul, 1969

Ready, O., in *East Anglian Reminiscences*, edited by Goodwyn, E. A., and Baxter, J. C., The Boydell Press, 1974

Reeve, L., *Farming on a Battle Ground*, Geo. R. Reeve, 1950

Reid, A., (ed.), *Cromer and Sheringham, the Growth of the Holiday Trade, 1877-1914*, Centre for East Anglian Studies, 1986

Richards, P., *King's Lynn*, Phillimore, 1990

Rider Haggard, H., *A Farmer's Year, being his commonplace book for 1898*, Cresset Library, 1899

Rider Haggard, L., *I Walked by Night*, Nicholson and Watson, 1935

Rider Haggard, L., *The Rabbit Skin Cap*, 1939, reprinted The Boydell Press, 1974

Rider Haggard, L., *Norfolk Life*, Alan Sutton, 1943

Rider Haggard, L., *Norfolk Notebook*, Alan Sutton, 1946

Rider Haggard, L., *A Country Scrapbook*, 1950, reprinted Alan Sutton, 1985

Rix, M., *Never Forget*, self-published, 1992

Robinson, B., *Passing Seasons*, Elmstead Publications, 1997

Roper, C., *Where the Birds Sing*, John Heywood, 1894

Serreau, A., *Times and Years: a history of the Blofield workhouse at Lingwood in the County of Norfolk*, Morrow and Co., 2000

de Soissons, M., *Brancaster Staithe - the story of a Norfolk fishing village*, Woodthorpe Publishing, 1993

Stone, R. W., 'Norfolk's World Beater' in *The Norfolk Magazine*, 1951

Storey, E., *North Bank Night*, Chatto and Windus, 1969

Storey, E., *A Man in Winter*, Chatto and Windus, 1972

Storey, E., *The Solitary Landscape*, Victor Gollancz, 1975

Sugden, C., and Kipper, S., *Prewd and Prejudice*, Mousehold Press, 1994

Sugden, C., and Kipper, S., *The Ballad of Sid Kipper*, Mousehold Press, 1996

Sugden, C., and Kipper, S., *Crab Wars*, Mousehold Press, 1999

Summers, D., *The Disaster: the East Coast Floods*, David and Charles, 1978

Tilbrook, R., *A Year in the Countryside*, Red Squirrels Publishing, 2000

Tooke, C., *Gorleston and Southtown*, Tookes Books, 1994

Tooley, B., *John Knowlittle: the Life of the Yarmouth Naturalist*, Wilson-Poole, 1985

Tusser, T., *Five Hundred Points of Good Husbandry, 1557*, reprinted Oxford University Press, 1984

Wallace, D., *Barnham Rectory*, Collins Clear-Type Press, 1934

Warren, C. H., *The Scythe in the Apple Tree*, Robert Hale, 1953
Wentworth Day, J., 'The King of Rockland Broad' in *East Anglian Magazine*, March 1976
Wesker, A., *As Much As I Dare*, Century, 1994
Westwood, J., *Gothick Norfolk*, Shire Publications, 1989
Williamson, H., *The Story of a Norfolk Farm*, Faber and Faber, 1941
Williamson, H., *Green Fields and Pavements*, 1941, reprinted by The Henry Williamson Society, 1995
Wilson, T. R., *Heartsease*, Headline, 1993
Woodforde, J., *A Country Parson: James Woodforde's Diary 1758-1802*, edited by Beresford, R. *et al.*, Oxford University Press, 1978
Wyer, S., *Requiem for a Village*, self-published, 1983
Yaxley, P., *Looking Back at Norfolk Cricket*, Nostalgia Publications, 1997
Yaxley, S. (ed.), *The Rector Will Be Glad - A Norfolk Parish Miscellany 1898-1920*, Larks Press, 1992